MAY   2015

Community Colleges

Arthur M. Cohen
EDITOR-IN-CHIEF

Caroline Q. Durdella
Nathan R. Durdella
ASSOCIATE EDITORS

Amy Fara Edwards
MANAGING EDITOR

D1529092

Dual Enrollment Policies, Pathways, and Perspectives

Jason L. Taylor
Joshua Pretlow
EDITORS

Number 169 • Spring 2015
Jossey-Bass
San Francisco

DUAL ENROLLMENT POLICIES, PATHWAYS, AND PERSPECTIVES
Jason L. Taylor, Joshua Pretlow (eds.)
New Directions for Community Colleges, no. 169

Arthur M. Cohen, Editor-in-Chief
Caroline Q. Durdella, Nathan R. Durdella, Associate Editors
Amy Fara Edwards, Managing Editor

NEW DIRECTIONS FOR COMMUNITY COLLEGES (ISSN 0194-3081, electronic ISSN 1536-0733) is part of The Jossey-Bass Higher and Adult Education Series and is published quarterly by Wiley Subscription Services, Inc., A Wiley Company, at Jossey-Bass, One Montgomery St., Ste. 1200, San Francisco, CA 94104. POSTMASTER: Send address changes to New Directions for Community Colleges, Jossey-Bass, One Montgomery St., Ste. 1200, San Francisco, CA 94104.

SUBSCRIPTIONS cost $89 for individuals in the U.S., Canada, and Mexico, and $113 in the rest of the world for print only; $89 in all regions for electronic only; $98 in the U.S., Canada, and Mexico for combined print and electronic; $122 for combined print and electronic in the rest of the world. Institutional print only subscriptions are $335 in the U.S., $375 in Canada and Mexico, and $409 in the rest of the world; electronic only subscriptions are $335 in all regions; combined print and electronic subscriptions are $402 in the U.S., $442 in Canada and Mexico, and $476 in the rest of the world.

Cover design: Wiley
Cover Images: © Lava 4 images | Shutterstock

EDITORIAL CORRESPONDENCE should be sent to the Editor-in-Chief, Arthur M. Cohen, at 1749 Mandeville Lane, Los Angeles, CA 90049. All manuscripts receive anonymous reviews by external referees.

New Directions for Community Colleges is indexed in CIJE: Current Index to Journals in Education (ERIC), Contents Pages in Education (T&F), Current Abstracts (EBSCO), Ed/Net (Simpson Communications), Education Index/Abstracts (H. W. Wilson), Educational Research Abstracts Online (T&F), ERIC Database (Education Resources Information Center), and Resources in Education (ERIC).

Microfilm copies of issues and articles are available in 16mm and 35mm, as well as microfiche in 105mm, through University Microfilms Inc., 300 North Zeeb Road, Ann Arbor, MI 48106-1346.

CONTENTS

EDITORS' NOTES

A Definitional Note on Dual Enrollment

We elected to use the term "dual enrollment" in the title of this volume and throughout the Editors' Notes. Dual enrollment is used in this volume to describe the general phenomenon of high school students enrolling in college-level courses other than exam-based courses such as Advanced Placement and International Baccalaureate. However, this term varies across state and institutional contexts and does not necessarily have the same meaning in every context. Alternative terms include "concurrent enrollment," "dual credit," and "postsecondary enrollment options." Although we use the term dual enrollment in the Editors' Notes of this volume, we purposefully requested that chapter authors use the term most relevant to their state and local contexts. The variation of terms used in this volume reflects the reality that multiple terms are used in policy and practice throughout the United States.

Introduction

There is no time like the present to take stock of dual enrollment programs in community colleges and institutions of higher education. This volume is timely for a number of reasons, including the evolving interest in dual enrollment by state policymakers, the increasing number of students participating in dual enrollment, and the relationship between dual enrollment and the college completion agenda.

It has been nearly 15 years since Robertson, Chapman, and Gaskin (2001) edited a volume of *New Directions for Community Colleges* (NDCC) on dual enrollment in which they identified dual enrollment as an emerging and powerful form of collaboration that has the potential to transform students' educational experiences and outcomes. As highlighted in this volume, the dual enrollment landscape has drastically transformed since 2001. Even since we began writing this volume in 2013, policy and practice have evolved in unique and somewhat unexpected ways at the federal, state, and local levels. For example, in spring 2014, the United States Department of Education released a solicitation of ideas for experimental sites for federal financial aid, and one example provided in the solicitation suggested that high school students could access federal financial aid for dual enrollment (as of January 2015, the financial aid experiments have not included dual enrollment). At the state level, the policy interest in dual enrollment is

NEW DIRECTIONS FOR COMMUNITY COLLEGES, no. 169, Spring 2015 © 2015 Wiley Periodicals, Inc.
Published online in Wiley Online Library (wileyonlinelibrary.com) • DOI: 10.1002/cc.20127

arguably at its highest point in history. The American Association of State Colleges and Universities' analysis of Gubernatorial State of the State addresses in 2014 found that dual enrollment and early colleges were the fourth most commonly discussed issue, just below college affordability/tuition policies (Harnisch & Parker, 2014).

The popularity of dual enrollment is partially grounded in an accumulating body of evidence that suggests dual enrollment is an effective strategy to support students' transition to and success in college. Rigorous evidence from several states (e.g., Florida, Illinois, New York, Texas) and one nationally representative study shows that relative to students who do not participate in dual enrollment, dual enrollment students are more likely to graduate high school (Karp, Calcagno, Hughes, Jeong, & Bailey, 2007), be prepared for college and participate in fewer remedial courses (An, 2013; Kim & Bragg, 2008), enroll in college (Karp et al., 2007; Struhl & Vargas, 2012; Taylor, 2013), persist in college and progress toward degree completion (Allen & Dadgar, 2012; Karp et al., 2007; Struhl & Vargas, 2012), and even complete college (An, 2013; Speroni, 2011; Struhl & Vargas, 2012; Taylor, 2013). Similarly, experimental results from the national early college impact study showed that students participating in early and middle college high schools had higher high school graduation and college enrollment rates than nonparticipants (Berger et al., 2013). Several of these studies elevate issues of equity, and we are learning more about how dual enrollment impacts different groups of students and may be a viable pathway for low-income students, students of color, first-generation students, and English language learners. This accumulating body of evidence is promising and has not gone unnoticed by educational leaders and policymakers. This body of rigorous evidence was nonexistent in 2001 when Robertson, Chapman, and Gaskin edited their *NDCC* volume, so the research base for dual enrollment has drastically expanded. Further, this research provides compelling evidence for strengthening and perhaps expanding dual enrollment programs, so a larger and more diverse group of students participate in and benefit from dual enrollment.

Despite this promising evidence, many of these studies make claims about dual enrollment without regard to variation in design and implementation. Whereas some studies account for key design dimensions and variation (e.g., course location, course type, course dosage, etc.), many studies disregard these design features and make broad claims about dual enrollment. Indeed, it is not uncommon for scholars and policymakers (ourselves included) to extrapolate research findings and make broad-based claims about dual enrollment's effectiveness without accounting for program design and state policy differences. This omission is not necessarily intentional but more likely reflects poorly designed data collection systems that preclude researchers from investigating the effects of various dual enrollment models on student outcomes. After all, dual enrollment operates at the junction between the secondary and postsecondary education systems in which many state and local data systems are structurally and legally separate. Implications for practice are that the research-based evidence regarding the relative impact of various dual enrollment models is largely absent when leaders and administrators consider how to design and execute dual enrollment programs and courses.

We believe the evidence on the impact of dual enrollment is critical to understanding program and policy effects, but this evidence is not the focus of this volume. Rather, the purpose of this volume is to examine dual enrollment models and contexts by highlighting diversity and variation in state policy and implementation, reviewing dual enrollment models and pathways for various student populations, surfacing key stakeholder perspectives, and considering issues of quality and institutional performance.

Reflecting on the Past

Before introducing the volume content to readers, it is valuable to briefly review the evolution of dual enrollment from a macro perspective. Early dual enrollment programs and courses predominately targeted students who were academically advanced. These programs and courses were often perceived and implemented as a pathway for academically gifted students who had exhausted their high school course options by senior year or before (Andrews, 2001; Andrews & Marshall, 1991). While academic dual enrollment courses were being delivered to academically gifted students, federal legislation supported the delivery of career and technical education (CTE) dual enrollment. The Carl D. Perkins Vocational and Applied Technology Education Act was passed in 1990, and this legislation for the first time integrated Tech Prep, a program designed to support CTE students' transition into postsecondary education and the workforce. Future reauthorizations of Perkins in 1998 and 2006 further strengthened Tech Prep and in particular the role of dual enrollment in Tech Prep programs.

Local implementation and federal Perkins legislation strengthened and expanded dual enrollment, but so did state policy. Andrews (2001) and the Education Commission of the States (2001) documented states' dual enrollment efforts at the turn of the century and found that nearly all states had some dual enrollment efforts at the state or institutional level. Karp, Bailey, Hughes, and Fermin's (2004) analysis of state policies revealed that 40 of the 50 states developed state policies that govern dual enrollment by 2003.

The first national estimate of the number of students participating in dual enrollment was documented during the 2002–2003 academic year when the National Center for Education Statistics (NCES) surveyed a nationally representative sample of public secondary schools and estimated there were 1.2 million students participating in dual enrollment (Waits, Setzer, & Lewis, 2005). NCES recently reproduced this survey, and, in the past decade, this number grew 66% to about 2.0 million dual enrollment students by the 2010–2011 academic year (Thomas, Marken, Gray, & Lewis, 2013).

Throughout the growth and evolution of dual enrollment, community colleges have been integral to the design and delivery of dual enrollment. Many state community college systems are the primary providers of dual enrollment (e.g., Arizona, California, Colorado, Illinois, Iowa, Virginia, Washington, etc.), and community colleges continue to be the largest postsecondary provider of dual enrollment nationally. NCES data show that 98% of community colleges provide dual enrollment courses to high school students, a percentage that is higher than any other postsecondary sector (Marken, Gray & Lewis, 2013). Further, community colleges are logical postsecondary partners for the delivery of dual enrollment because of their proximity to high schools and existing partnerships with high schools.

Purpose and Organization of the Volume

As dual enrollment policies and enrollments expand, so have the dual enrollment models, practices, and purposes. As a result of dual enrollment's expansion and maturation, dual enrollment is no longer exclusively a pathway for academically gifted students nor is it exclusively a pathway for CTE students under the guise of Tech Prep. Dual enrollment is not a monolithic phenomenon, but one that is characterized by variation in state policy intention, course and program design and focus, course location, course type, eligibility requirements, and its focus on the affective and noncognitive domain, among others. A primary purpose of this volume is to highlight this variation and feature a range of dual enrollment models that are designed to serve different student populations and create new pathways. In doing so, we hope this volume illustrates for readers how dual enrollment has matured and can serve as a pathway for both a greater number and more diverse group of students.

The volume is organized according to four major dimensions of dual enrollment: state policy, student pathways, stakeholder perspectives, and performance and evaluation. In Chapter 1, Taylor, Borden, and Park introduce readers to state dual enrollment policies and illustrate major policy dimensions and variation based on a national study. They point out that a majority of states have an explicit policy framework for dual enrollment that guides local policy and practice. Chapter 2 further illustrates how state policy influences local practice as Pretlow and Patteson draw from the experiences of a dual enrollment administrator to compare how state policies in Ohio and Virginia shape local actors and programs.

Chapters 3 through 5 feature how dual enrollment programs have created unique pathways for various student populations. Roach, Gamez Vargas, and David highlight Tulsa Community College's EXCELerate dual enrollment program in Chapter 3 and illustrate how the college navigated state and local policies to provide access to dual enrollment for students

NEW DIRECTIONS FOR COMMUNITY COLLEGES • DOI: 10.1002/cc

who are below state-mandated eligibility requirements. Their data on students' success support their efforts and have implications for how state policy, intentional or not, can prevent students in the academic middle from accessing college courses in high school. Chapter 4 introduces readers to Early and Middle College High School (E-MCHS) models in Michigan and New York and reviews how the states have created new pathways for students who historically have not accessed college, such as students of color, low-income students, English language learners, and first-generation college students. As Barnett, Maclutsky, and Wagonlander demonstrate, E-MCHSs themselves have evolved, yet they continue to embrace core principles that support students not only academically but also socially, psychologically, and behaviorally. In Chapter 5, Haag explores CTE dual enrollment and narrates her experiences as a dual enrollment administrator. This chapter draws attention to many of the unique dimensions of CTE dual enrollment, an understudied but large segment of many dual enrollment programs.

The next two chapters, Chapters 6 and 7, surface the voices and perspectives of key dual enrollment stakeholders: students and secondary representatives. In Chapter 6, Kanny reports results from a qualitative study of dual enrollment students in an urban charter school. Student perspectives often bring clarity to educational programs and policies, and Kanny's results help us better understand how students experience dual enrollment, what value students place on dual enrollment, and the challenges students experience with dual enrollment. In Chapter 7, we learn about the secondary perspective, a perspective overshadowed in the often postsecondary-dominated conversations related to dual enrollment. In this chapter, Hanson, Prusha, and Iverson share results from survey data that explore the perspectives of high school faculty, counselors, and principals.

The focus of the next two chapters shifts to issues related to student and program performance and evaluation. In Chapter 8, Ferguson, Baker, and Burnett unpack the construct of course rigor based on an analysis of faculty perspectives and course syllabi. In Chapter 9, Scheffel, McLemore, and Lowe draw from their experience at Lewis and Clark Community College to illustrate how dual enrollment accreditation through the National Association of Concurrent Enrollment Programs has strengthened local partnerships and how they navigated particular challenges associated with gaining and maintaining accreditation.

The final chapter in the volume is a thought piece written by Melinda Mechur Karp of the Community College Research Center at Teachers College, Columbia University. Karp has written and published extensively on dual enrollment and uses this chapter to argue that dual enrollment is a structural reform that can support the college completion agenda and contribute to more equitable educational outcomes.

Collectively, the chapters are a sampling of the landscape of dual enrollment research and practice in community colleges across the nation. Given the new developments in dual enrollment practice and policy over the past decade, we are eager to observe how dual enrollment continues to evolve and how dual enrollment might offer more pathways into higher education for a larger and more diverse group of students.

Jason L. Taylor
Joshua Pretlow
Editors

References

Allen, D., & Dadgar, M. (2012). Does dual enrollment increase students' success in college? Evidence from a quasi-experimental analysis of dual enrollment in New York City. In E. Hoffman & D. Voloch (Eds.), *New Directions for Higher Education: No. 158. Dual enrollment: Strategies, outcomes, and lessons for school–college partnerships* (pp. 11–19). San Francisco, CA: Jossey-Bass.

An, B. P. (2013). The impact of dual enrollment on college degree attainment: Do low-SES students benefit? *Educational Evaluation and Policy Analysis, 35*(1), 57–75.

Andrews, H. A. (2001). *The dual-credit phenomenon! Challenging secondary school students across 50 states.* Stillwater, OK: New Forums Press.

Andrews, H. A., & Marshall, R. P. (1991). Challenging high school honor students with community college courses. *Community College Review, 19*, 47–51.

Berger, A., Turk-Bicakci, L., Garet, M., Song, M., Knudson, J., Haxton, C., . . . Cassidy, L. (2013). *Early college, continued success: Early college high school initiative impact study.* Washington, DC: American Institutes for Research. Retrieved from http://www.air.org/resource/early-college-early-success-early-college-high-school-initiative-impact-study-2013

Education Commission of the States. (2001). *Postsecondary options: Dual/concurrent enrollment.* Retrieved from http://www.ecs.org/clearinghouse/28/11/2811.pdf

Harnisch, T. L., & Parker, E. A. (2014). *The 2014 Gubernatorial State of the State addresses and higher education.* Washington, DC: American Association of State Colleges and Universities. Retrieved from https://www.magnetmail.net/actions/email_web_version.cfm?message_id=3817560&user_id=AASCU

Karp, M. M., Bailey, T. R., Hughes, K. L., & Fermin, B. J. (2004). *State dual enrollment policies: Addressing access and quality.* Washington, DC: U.S. Department of Education.

Karp, M. M., Calcagno, J. C., Hughes, K. L., Jeong, D. W., & Bailey, T. R. (2007). *The postsecondary achievement of participants in dual enrollment: An analysis of student outcomes in two states.* New York, NY: Community College Research Center, Teachers College, Columbia University.

Kim, J., & Bragg, D. D. (2008). The impact of dual and articulated credit on college readiness and retention in four community colleges. *Career and Technical Education Research, 33*(2), 133–158.

Marken, S., Gray, L., & Lewis, L. (2013). *Dual enrollment programs and courses for high school students at postsecondary institutions: 2010–11* (NCES 2013-002). Washington, DC: National Center for Education Statistics, U.S. Department of Education. Retrieved from http://nces.ed.gov/pubs2013/2013002.pdf

Robertson, P. F., Chapman, B. G., & Gaskin, F. (Eds.). (2001). *New Directions for Community Colleges: No. 113. Systems for offering concurrent enrollment at high schools and community colleges.* San Francisco, CA: Jossey-Bass.

Speroni, C. (2011). *Determinants of students' success: The role of advanced placement and dual enrollment programs.* New York, NY: National Center for Postsecondary Research, Teachers College, Columbia University.

Struhl, B., & Vargas, J. (2012). *Taking college courses in high school: A strategy for college readiness—The college outcomes of dual enrollment in Texas.* Boston, MA: Jobs for the Future.

Taylor, J. L. (2013). *Community college dual credit: Differential participation and differential impacts on college access and success* (PhD dissertation). University of Illinois at Urbana-Champaign, Champaign, IL.

Thomas, N., Marken, S., Gray, L., & Lewis, L. (2013). *Dual credit and exam-based courses in U.S. public high schools: 2010–11* (NCES 2013-001). Washington, DC: National Center for Education Statistics, U.S. Department of Education. Retrieved from http://nces.ed.gov/pubs2013/2013001.pdf

Waits, T., Setzer, J. C., & Lewis, L. (2005). *Dual credit and exam-based courses in U.S. public high schools: 2002–03* (NCES 2005-009). Washington, DC: National Center for Education Statistics, U.S. Department of Education. Retrieved from http://nces.ed.gov/pubs2005/2005009.pdf

JASON L. TAYLOR *is an assistant professor of higher education in the Department of Educational Leadership and Policy at the University of Utah.*

JOSHUA PRETLOW *is an assistant professor of community college leadership at Old Dominion University in Norfolk, VA.*

1

This chapter reports results from a national policy study that examined state dual credit policies and how state policies address the quality of dual credit courses.

State Dual Credit Policy: A National Perspective

Jason L. Taylor, Victor H. M. Borden, Eunkyoung Park

Historically, the practice of offering college courses to high school students emerged from local practice in many states and was often initiated between local school and community college districts. In many states, this practice proceeded without clear state policy guidelines, regulations, or direction resulting in variation in local practice. Other states, such as Minnesota in the 1980s, were early adopters of state dual credit policy whereby state policy provided a framework for offering college courses to high school students. As dual enrollment, dual credit, and concurrent enrollment programs and courses grew, so have the state policies that regulate these courses and programs (we use the term dual credit in this chapter). Thus, local practices and programs described in several chapters in this volume are often contextualized, shaped, and constrained by the policies of the state in which they are located. Prior research has explored issues of access addressed in state policy components (Bragg, Kim, & Barnett, 2006; Education Commission of the States, 2001; Karp, Bailey, Hughes, & Fermin, 2004, 2005), but few have comprehensively examined issues of quality.

This chapter provides a national perspective on states' dual credit policies and reports results from a study that explored how state policies address quality.[1] The impetus for the study and interest in quality was based on the regional accrediting agencies' increasing interest in how quality is assured for dual credit courses. We sought to examine state policies to understand whether and how they regulate and ensure quality for the purpose of informing regional accrediting agencies.

General efforts to regulate and ensure dual credit quality have been approached in at least two ways. First, a national organization, the National Alliance of Concurrent Enrollment Partnerships (NACEP), is a voluntary organization from which high school and college partnerships seek

New Directions for Community Colleges, no. 169, Spring 2015 © 2015 Wiley Periodicals, Inc.
Published online in Wiley Online Library (wileyonlinelibrary.com) • DOI: 10.1002/cc.20128

accreditation status based on meeting quality standards through a process similar to program accreditation. According to NACEP's website, 92 "concurrent enrollment programs"[2] are NACEP-accredited (NACEP, 2014). Second, state policies have a role in maintaining the quality of dual credit programs. Karp et al.'s (2004, 2005) reviews of state dual credit policies illustrated how quality can be maintained via policies on student eligibility and through regulating course offerings. However, Karp et al. (2004, 2005) found less evidence of policies that address dual credit faculty professional development or academic and student support services for dual credit students (e.g., mentoring, study skills centers, and library facilities) that parallel those available to matriculated college students.

Despite the expansion of dual credit and growing concerns and attention to state policy ensuring the quality of dual credit, there is relatively little empirical research concerning the role of state policy in regulating and ensuring quality. The few studies that have been conducted at the national level found that there are large variations in dual credit policies ranging from nonexistent to extensive (Bragg et al., 2006; Education Commission of the States, 2001; Karp et al., 2004, 2005; Western Interstate Commission for Higher Education [WICHE], 2006). However, these studies did not provide an empirical analysis of dual credit state policies from a quality perspective. Toward this end, the purpose of this study is to address the following broad research questions regarding state dual credit policy:

1. What types and forms of dual credit courses can or cannot be offered?
2. Who is eligible and who is not eligible to enroll in dual credit offerings?
3. What criteria, if any, apply to instructors who teach dual credit courses?
4. What else is included in state policy that relates to ensuring the quality of dual credit course offerings (e.g., review processes, accountability, oversight provisions, etc.)?
5. How are state dual credit policies enforced?

We begin this chapter with a short review of the literature on prior dual credit policy studies and then report our results. We end the chapter by considering the implications of this study for community colleges and identifying key issues of consideration for community college administrators and faculty.

Prior Policy Reviews

Several of the national studies cited previously reviewed state dual credit policies, illustrating the wide variation, both in terms of policy approach and substance. At the time of their study, Karp et al. (2004, 2005) noted that 40 of the 50 states had dual enrollment legislative or regulatory policies. They described this variation according to 10 policy features: prescriptiveness (mandatory or voluntary), approach to oversight (financial reporting, policy compliance, or quality control), target population, admission requirements (student age, academics), location, student mix, instructor, course content, tuition, and funding. In their 2004 study, Karp et al. reported that policies related to student admission and finance were the most prevalent, whereas program structure was the least regulated. They attributed differences according to whether policy goals target academically advanced students or a wider range of students. Related to quality, the authors recommended that policymakers seek ways to "ensure the rigor of dual enrollment quality" (p. 32).

The Western Interstate Commission for Higher Education state policy study (WICHE, 2006) reported that dual enrollment was present in state statute or board policy in 42 states. The study focused on six dimensions of dual enrollment: student eligibility, application of course credit, carrying the cost burden, information sharing and counseling, institutional accountability, and incentives for success. Student eligibility was found to be the most common policy dimension, as in Karp et al.'s (2004, 2005) study. Also related to quality is what WICHE described as institutional accountability. They identified 10 states as having institutional accountability mechanisms in state policy and provided examples of these mechanisms that included annual reports to the legislature, joint accountability responsibilities for at-risk students, and inclusion of dual credit metrics in school performance reports.

Two salient themes emerge from these studies: (a) there is large variation in state policy, and (b) an emphasis on "quality" is underrepresented. A thorough review of dual credit quality is found in a more recent report from NACEP. In the report, Lowe (2010) described efforts underway in six states to oversee dual credit programs and align practice with quality standards. Lowe observed seven strategies for overseeing dual enrollment programs in these states including program approval, periodic program reviews, student outcome analysis, regular collegial meetings, course approvals, review of district/college MOUs, and annual reporting. Each of the six states in Lowe's report implemented at least two of these strategies with annual reporting the most common practice, observed in five of the six states. The current study extends the search for quality-related policy to all 50 states.

State Policy Review Methodology

This study employs a generic "input, process, output" (IPO) model as a framework to assess how state policy addresses dual credit quality and to ensure a balanced assessment of the components of quality as suggested by several scholars (Borden & Bottrill, 1994; Westerheijden, 2007). We identified the following aspects of inputs, processes, and outputs as they related to dual credit course quality:

- *Inputs*: student eligibility, faculty credentials, funding, and curriculum standards;
- *Processes*: general oversight, faculty orientation and training, institutional review and monitoring, and state review and monitoring;
- *Outputs*: learning outcomes, transferability, and program and course outcomes.

We used a combination of document analysis, a questionnaire, and structured interviews to document the ways in which policy in all 50 U.S. states addressed these three aspects of course quality. As with previous studies of dual credit policies (Karp et al., 2004, 2005), we focused on enumerated and written policies such as state legislation, state board or agency guidelines or procedures, or other state-mandated written policies. We used extant policy documents to initially complete a questionnaire, and we then conducted interviews with state agency and board officials to verify and adjust responses to the questionnaire. The interviews were conducted between spring 2012 and fall 2012. Representatives from all 50 states were included in the initial analysis, but Rhode Island and Utah did not respond to the inquiry, and Pennsylvania's program was recently defunded, so only 47 states were included in the final analysis.

Initially, most questionnaire items solicited simple "yes/no" responses accompanied by an opportunity to provide clarifying comments and policy language. We coded responses into four categories to reflect an overall level of prescriptiveness: (a) statewide requirement; (b) local requirement; (c) encouragement (either statewide or local); and (d) all other responses (no mention, nonspecific mention, or not applicable). One can conceptualize this scale as a continuum with "statewide requirement" at the highly prescriptive end of the spectrum and "all other responses" at the nonprescriptive end of the spectrum. Responses based on other formats were mapped to this general ordinal representation from the highest to lowest levels of prescriptiveness. Data were analyzed using descriptive statistics, mostly item frequency.

Results

A graphical representation of the frequency responses is discussed next and is displayed in Figure 1.1 and Figure 1.2. Detailed results of the study, including state-by-state profiles, are available on the Higher Learning Commission's website.[3]

Course Provisions.   Thirty-four of the 47 states (72%) had some policy regulating the types of dual credit courses that can be offered, 27 of which were state requirements. The most frequent policy in this area was

Figure 1.1.   Response Frequencies, Course Offerings, and Student
Eligibility

Course Offerings	Statewide Requirement		Local Requirement		
	Encouragement		No or Nonspecific Mention		
	0 10 20		30 40 50		
Any regulations on course offerings	27		1 6 13		
Subject matter restrictions	20	1 4	22		
Statewide transfer requirements	18	3	26		
Requirement for high schools to make available	10	7	30		
Requirement for public colleges to offer	5 1 8		33		
Statewide general education requirements	7 1		39		
Other restrictions	4 1		42		
Minimum or maximum number of restrictions	3 1		43		
Student Eligibility	0 10 20		30 40 50		
Any regulations on student eligibility	27		7 3 10		
Class level requirement	28		1 4 14		
Exam requirements	13	9 3	22		
Course prerequisites	12	10 2	23		
Exceptions or waivers allowed	13	3 4	27		
Other restrictions	15	2 2	28		
Minimum/maximum credit restrictions	14	3	30		
Marketing of dual credit options	14	1 1	31		
GPA requirement	13	2 1	31		
Registration timing restrictions	7 3		37		
Age requirement	3 1		43		

related to the subject or discipline of dual credit courses. For example, Massachusetts and Georgia policies explicitly prohibited remedial or developmental courses, as did Oklahoma and Kansas. Kansas's policy connected course type to funding, noting that remedial coursework that does not apply toward an approved program is ineligible for financial reimbursement.

Two additional common features of state policy were the transferability and availability of courses. Related to the former, some state policies indicated that courses needed to be in the state transfer system or library or otherwise part of institutional articulation agreements, as is the case in Arkansas and Indiana, for example. Related to the latter, we found that five states require colleges to offer dual credit, 10 states require high schools to have dual credit options, and seven states encourage high schools to have dual credit options. In the majority of states, however, offering dual credit was a voluntary local decision.

Student Eligibility.   One of the most prevalent dimensions of state policy was policy language about which students can participate in dual credit; nearly 80% ($n = 37$) of state policies regulated dual credit student eligibility. This ranged from policies dictating high school students' class level (33 states), to exam requirements (25 states), to GPA requirements

Figure 1.2.   Response Frequencies, Instructor Eligibility, and Quality Assurance

Instructor Eligibility	Statewide Requirement	Local Requirement	Encouragement	No or Nonspecific Mention
Any regulations on instructor eligibility	27	7	3	10
Same criteria as for on-campus instructors	22	7	2	16
Instructor selection process requirements	15	6	1	25
Subject matter degree/experience	14	2	2	29
Specified degree level	13	1	3	30
Ongoing professional development requirements	9	3	5	30
Prior training requirements	9	1	4	33
Exceptions or waivers allowed	5	3		39
Other restrictions	2	1	3	41

Quality Assurance	Statewide Requirement	Local Requirement	Encouragement	No or Nonspecific Mention
Course rigor provisions	10	22		15
Partnership regulations	21	11		24
Registration/transcripting requirements	17	5		25
Support service provisions	14	1	5	27
Other faculty interaction requirements	5	5	6	31
Outcome monitoring provisions	12	3	1	31
Catalog requirements	9	2	2	34
College oversights regulations	6	4	3	34
Classroom visitations	7	5		35
Other forms of monitoring	7	1		39
Minimum grade for credit requirements	2	4		41
Stakeholder survey provisions	1	1	3	42

(16 states). Very common and evident in 25 states were policy provisions for exam or course prerequisites that often dictated colleges use the same eligibility criteria for dual credit as are used for all college students. Results also showed that 20 states had policy language that allowed exceptions or waivers for dual credit eligibility requirements. For example, Kentucky policy stated, "Exceptions may be considered for other students if recommended by the school faculty and approved by the Chief Academic Officer at the public postsecondary institution."

Instructor Eligibility.   Also common in state policies were regulations related to who can teach dual credit courses; nearly 80% ($n = 37$) of state policies included a provision. A preponderance of policies (31 of the 37), exemplified by Maryland, state that course instructors "shall meet the same requirements for appointment as regular faculty at the collegiate institution granting the credit." Indeed, this is a general provision of most institution's accreditation standards and sometimes this connection is explicit in state policy as noted in Missouri policy, which states that instructor selection "shall meet the requirements … as stipulated for accreditation by the Higher Learning Commission." A smaller although still sizeable number of states had policy language that required instructors to have specific courses (18 states) or have earned a master's degree in a specific discipline (17 states).

About one third of states had policy provisions pertaining to prior training and ongoing professional development for faculty. For example, 14 states had requirements that dual credit faculty receive training before teaching, and 17 states had policies that require ongoing professional development for dual credit faculty.

Other Quality Assurance Provisions. We examined a number of other state policy provisions including accreditation requirements, annual reporting requirements, and partnership regulations. For example, eight states had policies that either require or encourage NACEP or an equivalent form of accreditation, and 30 states had annual reporting requirements related to dual credit. Several other quality provisions were examined, and we found evidence of the following provisions: course rigor (32 states), partnership regulations (23 states), support service (20 states), other requirements for faculty interaction (16 states), student outcome monitoring (16 states), classroom visitation (12 states), and stakeholder survey (5 states).

Of considerable interest to the research community is the extent to which policy requires reporting on dual credit or dual credit students, which affects the ways in which scholars and policymakers alike have access to data to study dual credit. Our results found that 30 states have annual reporting requirements on dual credit, but only 16 states have policies requiring or encouraging monitoring student outcomes.

Policy Enforcement. Language about policy enforcement was generally very limited in state dual credit policies, but when asked about policy enforcement, respondents often noted that general state compliance provisions were used to enforce policy. In some states, dual credit was the subject of agency accounting or auditing processes. For example, the Commonwealth of Virginia does not regulate who can take dual credit courses, but colleges within the Virginia Community College System were subject to the requirements and policies of the State Board for Community Colleges and were subject to their internal audit process. Other states also employed auditing as a mechanism for enforcement. For example, in Texas dual credit was the subject of an audit by the State Auditor's Office and passed through the process successfully in 2010.

Implications for Community Colleges

We conclude this chapter with a discussion of implications for community colleges and review issues that community college administrators and faculty should consider as they relate to state dual credit policy. It is particularly important to emphasize that state policies establish the parameters for local practice. It follows that the program goals, assumptions, and design at the local level should reflect the state level, assuming local policy enactment aligns with written policy.

Access.   Consistent with the community college open-access mission, national data show that 98% of public two-year institutions offer dual credit courses, higher than any other institutional type (Thomas, Marken, Gray, & Lewis, 2013). While these data might suggest that dual credit is highly accessible via the community college sector, our study suggests that restrictions on student eligibility are among the most common dimension of state policy. In some states, state-level eligibility criteria are restrictive, or colleges have established relatively high student eligibility requirements to ensure quality, yet the criteria are not necessarily grounded in research and best practice. Establishing arbitrary placement cutoff scores may actually restrict access for students who most need access, and some dual credit programs, such as the EXCELerate program highlighted by Roach, Gamez Vargas, and David in this volume, demonstrate students can be successful if given the opportunity and are supported in their learning.

Many state policies require dual credit programs to be well publicized or integrated into student planning documents, and this is a sound practice that supports students' access. Those students least likely to be aware of dual credit or understand registration and eligibility requirements are arguably the students who may have the most to benefit from participating in college courses while in high school. Practices aimed at increasing awareness and expanding eligibility to ensure dual credit access are in the spirit of community colleges' historical mission.

Course Transferability.   The transferability of dual credit courses (or lack thereof) is of considerable concern and interest in many states. Many high school students receive college credit for dual credit courses from community colleges that students do not plan to attend after high school graduation. Our study shows that only about half of state policies address the transferability of dual credit courses, and Pretlow and Patteson's chapter in this volume further illustrates challenges associated with the transfer of dual credit courses. Although many states have developed and implemented statewide transfer policies to support the transferability of community college courses and students, receiving institutions may have discretion to accept or deny community college dual credit courses if state dual credit policy does not explicitly require that courses transfer. There are many anecdotes of elite private and public universities, for example, that choose not to accept students' dual credit courses as transferable even though courses are in state transfer agreements and policies. The acceptance of community college dual credit courses by universities signals to students, parents, and policymakers that dual credit courses are high quality and meet quality standards established by state transfer policies.

More research is needed on dual credit course transferability to understand how many and which courses are transferable, barriers to dual credit transferability, and if existing state policies are adequate to ensure dual credit transfer. Community colleges can and should survey former dual credit students to ask about how students' dual credit courses transferred. In the absence of state policies regulating transfer, community colleges can also contact public and private universities to inquire about university transfer policies related to dual credit to ensure that students' credits are accepted by universities.

Partnerships and Faculty Engagement. An integral element of dual credit is successful partnerships with high schools, and many state dual credit policies require that colleges and high schools establish strong partnerships that require regular engagement and interactions among college and high school faculty. Community colleges are particularly accustomed to engaging with high school faculty and administrators in the context of career and technical education (CTE). For example, the federal Carl D. Perkins legislation that funds CTE requires high schools and colleges to develop a seamless program of study that spans the 9th to 14th grades, and many CTE high school and college faculty engage regularly in curriculum development and alignment. State dual credit policies can support and reinforce existing CTE partnerships and extend these partnerships into academic courses. One outcome of Perkins legislation is that high school and community college CTE courses are well aligned and provide students a smooth transition between high school and college. Engagement between high school and community college academic faculty may lead to similar benefits whereby high school and community college faculty have a more detailed understanding of their counterparts' teaching philosophy, student expectations, curriculum, pedagogy, and assessment. Thus, dual credit policies simultaneously have the potential to improve alignment between high school and college and to increase dual credit course quality.

Accompanying the expanded partnerships and increased engagement are the human and fiscal resources needed to initiate and sustain these activities. However, many state policies do not allocate additional funding to high schools or colleges to support partner and engagement activities (Borden, Taylor, Park, & Seiler, 2013). For community colleges that already receive the smallest share of state funding among public institutions of higher education (Mullin, 2010), compliance with these state policies may come at an increased cost to institutions as an unfunded mandate. Community colleges should lobby for the human and fiscal resources needed to meet state policy goals, providing evidence of the positive alignment outcomes that result from partner engagement.

State Mandates, Regional Accreditation, and Local Variation. Like state policy, regional accreditation also sets parameters and limits within which community college dual credit programs and practices can vary. Regional accreditation criteria only indirectly address dual credit, and are intended to govern dual credit programs as they do all college programs— to ensure program and course quality. The accreditation criteria reinforce many state dual credit policies or supplement state policies by holding colleges to high standards for courses taught on high schools or in other contracted education that is not on the college campus, for example.

Accreditation criteria can occasionally conflict with state policy, however, and both support and challenge institutions regarding issues of autonomy and possibilities for innovation. For example, most regional accreditation criteria include provisions that students have access to adequate support services, but many state dual credit policies do not require support services for dual credit students and consequently many institutions do not offer them. No doubt, extending services such as library access, tutoring, writing centers, etc., to all high school students taking college courses (including online college courses) is a challenging endeavor for many institutions, especially those that have dual credit agreements with dozens of high school partners.

As dual credit programs continue to expand and scale throughout the nation, community college leaders and administrators need to consider how both state policy and regional accreditation criteria intersect, converge, and diverge when constructing local dual credit policies. Similarly, state policymakers should be sensitive to how state dual credit policies influence institutional obligations to regional accreditors. Finally, regional accrediting agencies should recognize how their accreditation criteria related to dual credit might need to be refined so institutions and states can clearly interpret and understand accreditor expectations; the Higher Learning Commission released dual credit guidelines for institutions in 2013 that began to address accreditor expectations for dual credit.

Notes

1. The research presented in this chapter was sponsored by the Higher Learning Commission of the North Central Association of Colleges and Schools (HLC) on behalf of the Council for Regional Accreditation Commissions and with support from the Lumina Foundation.

2. The terms used to characterize dual credit vary, with concurrent enrollment, dual credit, and dual enrollment being the most common. We use the term dual credit unless referring to the term used formally by an organization, such as NACEP in this case.

3. As of the publication date of this chapter, the direct link to the full report was available at https://www.ncahlc.org/Pathways/dual-credit-programs-and-courses.html

References

Borden, V. M. H., & Bottrill, K. (1994). Performance indicators: History, definitions, and methods. In V. M. H. Borden & T. W. Banta (Eds.), *New Directions for Institutional Research: No. 82. Using performance indicators to guide strategic decision making* (pp. 5–21). San Francisco, CA: Jossey-Bass.

Borden, V. M. H., Taylor, J. L., Park, E., & Seiler, D. J. (2013). *Dual credit in U.S. higher education: A study of state policy and quality assurance practices.* Chicago, IL: Higher Learning Commission.

Bragg, D. D., Kim, E., & Barnett, E. A. (2006). Creating access and success: Academic pathways reaching underserved students. In D. D. Bragg & E. A. Barnett (Eds.), *New*

Directions for Community Colleges: No. 135. Academic pathways to and from the community college (pp. 5–19). San Francisco, CA: Jossey-Bass.

Education Commission of the States. (2001). *Postsecondary options: Dual and concurrent enrollment.* Denver, CO: Author.

Karp, M. M., Bailey, T. R., Hughes, K. L., & Fermin, B. J. (2004). *State dual enrollment policies: Addressing access and quality.* Washington, DC: U.S. Department of Education.

Karp, M. M., Bailey, T. R., Hughes, K. L., & Fermin, B. J. (2005). *Update to state dual enrollment policies: Addressing access and equity.* New York, NY: Community College Research Center, Teachers College, Columbia University.

Lowe, A. L. (2010). *Promoting quality: State strategies for overseeing dual enrollment programs.* Chapel Hill, NC: National Alliance of Concurrent Enrollment Partnerships.

Mullin, C. M. (2010, June). *Rebalancing the mission: The community college completion challenge* (Policy Brief 2010-02PBL). Washington, DC: American Association of Community Colleges.

National Alliance of Concurrent Enrollment Partnerships (NACEP). (2014). *NACEP's history.* Retrieved from http://www.nacep.org/about-nacep/history/

Thomas, N., Marken, S., Gray, L., & Lewis, L. (2013). *Dual credit and exam-based courses in U.S. public high schools: 2010–11* (NCES 2013-001). Washington, DC: National Center for Education Statistics, U.S. Department of Education.

Westerheijden, D. F. (2007). States and Europe and quality of higher education. *Quality Assurance in Higher Education, 20,* 73–95.

Western Interstate Commission for Higher Education (WICHE). (2006, June). *Accelerated learning options: Moving the needle on access and success. A study of state and institutional policies and practices.* Boulder, CO: Author.

Jason L. Taylor is an assistant professor of higher education in the Department of Educational Leadership and Policy at the University of Utah.

Victor H. M. Borden is a professor of educational leadership and policy studies at Indiana University Bloomington.

Eunkyoung Park is an associate research fellow at the Korean Educational Development Institute.

2

This chapter investigates the consequences and implications of dual enrollment policy diversity on operating dual enrollment programs in the two states of Ohio and Virginia.

Operating Dual Enrollment in Different Policy Environments: An Examination of Two States

Joshua Pretlow, Jennifer Patteson

Dual enrollment programs have grown significantly over the past decade to the point where almost all community colleges offer some form of dual enrollment (Marken, Gray, & Lewis, 2013). This is encouraging news for both the growing number and diversity of students who avail themselves of the opportunity to earn college-level credits while still in high school. While dual enrollment and its associated growth have received much deserved attention, the role of state policy in shaping dual enrollment programs has not received equal treatment. As Chapter 1 by Taylor, Borden, and Park illustrates, what we mean by dual enrollment varies tremendously by state. Likewise, the policies, or lack of policies, in states shape how operators of dual enrollment programs can structure and implement programs on the local level. This state-by-state policy diversity is evident when one peruses the Education Commission of the States (ECS) dual enrollment database (ECS, 2013).

This chapter investigates the consequences and implications of dual enrollment policy diversity in two states. We first briefly present the state-level dual enrollment policy context in Ohio and Virginia and note similarities and differences. We then draw on the lived experiences of a dual enrollment coordinator who has worked in each of these two states in order to critically examine the consequences—both positive and negative—that certain policies or lack of policies create. We examine these consequences from three stakeholders' perspectives—higher education, secondary education, and students—as policies can and often do create conflicting incentives among stakeholder groups (Stone, 2012). Since policies are not

New Directions for Community Colleges, no. 169, Spring 2015 © 2015 Wiley Periodicals, Inc.
Published online in Wiley Online Library (wileyonlinelibrary.com) • DOI: 10.1002/cc.20129

static, we should note that we will be discussing state-level policy for the periods of 2008–2010 in Virginia and 2012–2013 in Ohio. We conclude by recommending general principles that policymakers should consider when crafting new or revising existing dual enrollment policy.

State Dual Enrollment Policy Context: Ohio and Virginia

In order to understand the system under which dual enrollment operates in each state, we first need to discuss the policies themselves. On a macro level, both Virginia and Ohio policies sanction dual enrollment programs that allow qualified students to simultaneously earn both high school and college credits for successfully completing qualified courses offered on either a high school or a college campus. Other than this generalized framework, the policy differences are both substantial and significant. The first main difference is that Virginia operates under the Virginia Plan for Dual Enrollment (VPDE, 2008), which is updated periodically—most recently in March of 2008—and signed by the chancellor of the Virginia Community College System (VCCS), Secretary of Education, and the Superintendent of Public Instruction. The VPDE provides stakeholders a centralized framework related to dual enrollment policy in Virginia. Alternatively, Ohio lacks a central repository of information related to dual enrollment policy and procedures. This forces stakeholders to search out bits and pieces of information from myriad sources.

Regarding policies governing the implementation of dual enrollment programs, Virginia and Ohio differ on many aspects. The most prominent difference is that all dual enrollment in Virginia is offered through the 23 institutions that the VCCS comprises, while any accredited Ohio postsecondary institutions, including for-profit institutions, can offer dual enrollment courses. In Virginia this distinct service area philosophy has created a situation in which school districts and individual high schools know who is responsible for dual enrollment in their area. Contrast this to Ohio where high schools can have more than one—and sometimes three, four, or five—postsecondary institutions offering dual enrollment courses in their high school building. This difference in defined service areas is emblematic of other differences in the two states as well.

Student eligibility in Virginia is generally limited to high school juniors and seniors with special exceptions granted for freshmen and sophomores whereas Ohio's program is open to all high school students with a high school grade point average of 3.0 or higher. Rather than relying on high school grade point average, student eligibility in Virginia is determined by a student being accepted into college-level courses based on the placement exam in that subject area and a recommendation from the student's high school. Although dual enrollment opportunities in Ohio appear to be open to a greater number of students than in Virginia, each postsecondary institution in Ohio can mandate further eligibility requirements for students.

Examples of further requirements utilized in Ohio include placement testing, specific high school prerequisite courses, and grades.

The cost to students to participate in a dual enrollment course is an important programmatic feature. In Ohio, financing is a local decision and postsecondary institutions are free to set tuition rates for dual enrollment students at any level as long as that rate is approved by the Ohio Board of Regents (OBR). Further, the state reimburses only the postsecondary institution for a participating student. In Virginia, the state "encourages" offering dual enrollment at no cost to students by giving both the high school and community college full credit in the state funding formulas for each dual enrolled student. Whereas some deride this funding practice as "double dipping" (Hoffman, 2005, p. 15), we argue that the state is simply paying earlier, rather than twice, for this college course. Faculty credentialing is also decentralized in Ohio. Although the OBR guides local decisions on faculty credentialing, each postsecondary institution determines who is qualified to teach a particular dual enrollment course at a high school. Virginia relies on the credentialing criteria established by their accrediting board, the Southern Association of Colleges and Schools.

A final difference to note is the transfer of earned dual enrollment credit. In a reversal of what one would expect from the descriptions thus far, Ohio's transfer policy is more centralized and uniform than Virginia's policy. Ohio has designated certain courses as being "Ohio Transfer Module" (OTM) or "Transfer Assurance Guarantee" (TAG). A course with the OTM designation means that all public institutions will accept the credits and count them toward general education requirements. TAG-designated courses are degree-specific courses and are accepted in fulfillment of major requirements (Ohio Board of Regents, 2010). Certain courses can carry both designations and thus satisfy both a general education and a major-specific requirement. In contrast, dual enrollment credits are treated as community college credits in Virginia. This means that credits can be transferred to a four-year institution only if that accepting institution permits it. Since specific four-year institutions require specific courses to fulfill general education and major requirements, this can become problematic. For example, one four-year institution may accept Math 163 as fulfilling a general education math requirement, while another institution may not accept Math 163 but require Math 164.

Market and Centralized Approaches.   As is evident from the preceding description, there are both positive and negative aspects of Ohio's and Virginia's dual enrollment policies. In general, Ohio's policy is more decentralized and gives more discretion to localities and individual institutions than does Virginia's policy. The dual enrollment coordinator interviewed for this chapter confirmed this as she consistently used phrases such as "free market" and "free for all" when referring to Ohio. In contrast, when discussing Virginia, she used the words "standardized" and "centralized." Her characterization of the two state's policies, combined with an examination of the policies themselves, leads us to label Ohio's dual enroll-ment program a "market" approach and Virginia's a "centralized" approach. While acknowledging that each state falls on a continuum and contains as-pects of centralization and decentralization, we feel that our characteriza-tion is accurate. We will utilize these terms to refer to the respective states for the remainder of this chapter in which we discuss the benefits and draw-backs of each approach and then provide recommendations.

Methods and Limitations

We rely on the lived experiences of one dual enrollment coordinator who worked at two postsecondary institutions in the two states and time peri-ods under examination. The dual enrollment coordinator was interviewed on two occasions and reviewed the written manuscript. Her responses were coded and analyzed by the two-step process described in Coffey and Atkin-son (1996). On the first read, general themes were noted. Second, these gen-eral themes were used to develop more precise codes that were applied to the data. We coded both confirming and disconfirming evidence. Although this study provides rich data based on the experiences of one individual at two colleges, personnel at other institutions in those states may have had a different experience.

Findings

Policy implementation does not strictly follow written policy. Integrating the macro and micro actors—state-level policymakers and dual enrollment administrators, respectively—is a difficult process (McLaughlin, 1987). The process of translating policy into actionable programs is further complicated when a policy is vaguely written or not found in an accessible location. Our findings indicate that Ohio exemplifies these issues to a greater extent than does Virginia.

   Clarity.   Our first finding that is dominant throughout the interviews with the dual enrollment administrator is the theme of clarity. She cites ex-amples from both states in which an ambiguous policy results in confusion for her, the institutions, and the students. For example, students and parents in Virginia were confused by the transferability of dual enrollment courses to other institutions of postsecondary education. From the parents' and stu-dents' point of view, it is a seemingly idiosyncratic decision that one public institution would only accept Math 163 and another 164 to fulfill a general education requirement. This situation can limit students' college-going op-tions and in some instances force them to decide on course taking without knowing if they will be admitted to a particular four-year institution.

   In contrast, Ohio has a clear transfer system in which specific courses are labeled as either OTM or TAG or both. These include not just gen-eral education courses but major-specific courses as well. These courses are outlined on the University System of Ohio's website. In addition to providing clarity to the parents and students, this clear transfer of credits also eases the burden on an already overworked group—high school and community college counselors. To effectively advise high school students in Virginia on dual enrollment options, a counselor has to know which courses each four-year institution in Virginia will and will not accept. This creates unreal expectations for counselors. Although there is a constant chorus to increase the number of counselors at both high schools and community colleges (Edwards, 2011), simply increasing the number will not alleviate this issue. Rather, policy changes at the state level clarifying the transfer of dual enrollment credits are needed. If the transfer of dual enrollment credits is not specifically addressed and is simply treated as any community college credit, there is a risk that high school guidance counselors are effectively being tasked with advising students on transfer issues. This situation has the potential to harm students if they receive incorrect information.

The theme of clarity emerged in another area related to dual enrollment policy. Since Virginia operates dual enrollment exclusively through its community colleges, there is one well-defined postsecondary institution associated with each school district and high school. Further, each community college has an established dual enrollment contact who is listed on the VCCS website. Alternatively, Ohio operates under the market system and has no defined dual enrollment service areas. The lack of a defined service area allows high schools to partner with more than one postsecondary institution to offer dual enrollment courses. The result is that some high schools partner with four or five postsecondary institutions to offer dual enrollment courses in the same semester. The dual enrollment coordinator provided an example from one Ohio high school where two postsecondary institutions offered dual enrollment chemistry in the same semester. Combined with the different tuition each institution requires, parents and students at this high school were confused as to which institution offered what dual enrollment course and why the cost of the courses varied. Along with allowing students to earn college-level credit, dual enrollment programs have been touted as increasing the relationships and cooperation between high schools and colleges, two historically distinct sectors (Kirst & Bracco, 2004). Espoused benefits of an increased relationship include the vertical alignment of curriculum. When a single high school has multiple partner institutions offering dual enrollment in one subject area, the benefit of curriculum alignment can be lost.

Cooperation.   Many policies attempt to balance the interests of diverse stakeholders' competing priorities. Two common examples are the balance often sought between equity and efficiency and security and liberty (Stone, 2012). In the two states under investigation, dual enrollment policy is situated between the opposing demands of cooperation and competition. With its emphasis on markets, Ohio's policy embraces competition over cooperation, while Virginia's policy prioritizes cooperation. These different foci and the resulting consequences for operating a dual enrollment program were evident to the dual enrollment coordinator. She reported that working under Virginia's policy resulted in a more cooperative relationship with her dual enrollment administrator colleagues at other community colleges. She gave two specific examples of this. First, she reported that it was "easier when you knew you had a group of people" who could be called upon when you encountered an issue. Not only was this group of people, her dual credit colleagues at the other community colleges, listed on the VCCS website but she also attended an annual daylong meeting of all dual enrollment coordinators sponsored by the VCCS. The personal relationships she developed at the annual meeting allowed her to feel more comfortable in reaching out to these individuals.

The second example the dual enrollment coordinator provided combines the advantage of cooperation in Virginia and the disadvantage of competition in Ohio. Although there was no sponsored group of dual enrollment coordinators in Ohio, she was able to locate contact information for coordinators after searching institutional websites. However, the lack of defined service areas created a disincentive for cooperation among her colleagues. She reported that the philosophy was one of competition and that the lack of a defined service area resulted in some dual enrollment administrators adopting the mindset of "why meet and talk about best practices when if I'm doing something great I'm going to get that enrollment and the money from it?" She went on to say that institutions "want to have a competitive edge" in the competition for students. The competition for dual enrollment students and their resulting revenue, especially in a state in which the number of traditional college age students is declining (WICHE, 2013), was a real issue.

Instrumental to the competitive environment in Ohio was that each postsecondary institution established its own dual enrollment tuition rates that ranged from $0 to $180 per credit hour. This competition on tuition may result in lower rates for students, which can be a positive benefit of the market approach. The dual credit coordinator reported that some postsecondary institutions went so far as to call high schools to determine what other institutions were charging and then work with a high school to offer courses at a lower rate for students. This can be beneficial for students and families. However, it is not known whether this competition for students based on tuition rates compensates for the accompanying lack in cooperation, especially if best practices are not widely shared. Although beneficial for the student in terms of slightly reduced tuition and for the postsecondary institution in terms of increased enrollment and revenue, if the effectiveness of dual enrollment as a whole is compromised, the state ultimately suffers. The state benefits when more individuals access and achieve success in postsecondary education, not when one institution increases their enrollment by 20 students and another loses 20 students, as this is not a net gain for the state. Rather, the state benefits when the greatest number of students experience the most effective dual enrollment course and continue on to earn a postsecondary credential. As currently structured, the state policy in Ohio is not encouraging the stated statewide goal of increasing the postsecondary completion rate.

Recommendations for Policy

Dual enrollment as a practice that has the potential to help ease the transition from high school to college for a growing number of students has received increased attention in recent years. However, state-level policies that shape dual enrollment programs have not received equal treatment. Our piece compared the lived experiences of one dual enrollment administrator who had worked in both Ohio and Virginia. An examination of each state's policies combined with her assessment of operating a dual enrollment program under those guidelines lead us to label Ohio as a "market" approach and Virginia as a "centralized" approach. There are positive and negative aspects to each approach and we draw from those to provide policy recommendations that can lead to more effective programs for all students.

In discussing dual enrollment policy, we would be remiss if we did not explicitly acknowledge the uniqueness of dual enrollment at the intersection of secondary schools, community colleges, and four-year institutions. Policy governing dual enrollment has to consider all three of these disparate sectors of education—in addition to academic and career and technical education programs—and to appease this diverse constituency; this is not an easy task. With that in mind, we argue that dual enrollment policy should seek to be clear to all stakeholders, promote cooperation among sectors, and ensure equity for equal participation.

Our first recommendation is that each state should have a clear policy that addresses all relevant areas of dual enrollment and can be found in one location or document. This will not only ease the burden on dual enrollment administrators and students, but will also allow policymakers to consider dual enrollment policy as a whole rather than as a sum of its disconnected parts. When policy is developed or refined in an ad hoc fashion, a small change to one aspect can have ripple effects in other unintended areas. Likewise, if dual enrollment policy is simply the extension of standard postsecondary policies, unique issues may arise. As the example of Virginia illustrates, applying existing policy on the transfer of community college credits to dual enrollment credits has the unintended consequence of burdening high school guidance counselors with additional advising responsibilities. To prevent scenarios such as these, dual enrollment policy should be considered both as a whole and distinct from existing postsecondary policy, not separate policy related to financing, access, transfer of credits, and service areas, just to name a few of the interrelated aspects.

Second, policy related to dual enrollment should promote cooperation among educational sectors and institutions. To be an effective statewide

NEW DIRECTIONS FOR COMMUNITY COLLEGES • DOI: 10.1002/cc

strategy for increasing college access and success, dual enrollment policy needs to be designed to serve that end. The state, through the development and implementation of a comprehensive statewide dual enrollment policy, has the potential to increase both college access and success. However, when dual enrollment policy is structured to reward single institution behaviors, as is the case in Ohio, the incentive to cooperate among institutions is lost. When cooperation turns to competition for students and their tuition dollars, dual enrollment has the potential to be viewed as an institutional revenue source. If this is the case, individual institutions are encouraged to enroll as many students as possible, even if there is no net gain for the state in terms of the total number of participating students.

Third, dual enrollment policy should promote equitable participation from all groups of students (Pretlow & Wathington, 2014). As research is beginning to demonstrate, dual enrollment can be an effective transition tool for many students other than the traditional high achieving student. However, for a state to use it effectively to that end, it has to be both available and known to a greater number of students. The issues noted above around transfer of credit, pricing, and service areas can be more difficult to understand for those students with less college knowledge, often low-income and first-generation students. If dual enrollment is to successfully serve all students and provide an "on-ramp" from high school to postsecondary education, all stakeholders need to fully understand aspects of the program and policies which govern it. If students or institutional actors are unclear, there is an increased risk for nonparticipation or unwise decisions. A comprehensive, clear, and accessible statewide policy can go a long way toward eliminating these hurdles.

References

Coffey, A., & Atkinson, P. (1996). *Making sense of qualitative data: Complimentary research strategies.* New York, NY: Sage.

Education Commission of the States (ECS). (2013, December). *Dual enrollment—All state profiles.* Retrieved from http://ecs.force.com/mbdata/mbprofallRT?Rep=DE13A

Edwards, J. (2011). *Survey of community/2 year college counseling services.* American College Counseling Association. Retrieved from http://www.collegecounseling.org/docs/ACCA-CCTF-2011SurveyBooklet.pdf

Hoffman, N. (2005, April). *Add and subtract: Dual enrollment as a state strategy to increase postsecondary success for underrepresented students.* Boston, MA: Jobs for the Future. Retrieved from http://files.eric.ed.gov/fulltext/ED497806.pdf

Kirst, M. W., & Bracco, K. R. (2004). Bridging the great divide. In M. W. Kirst & A. Venezia (Eds.), *From high school to college: Improving opportunities for success in postsecondary education* (pp. 1–30). San Francisco, CA: Jossey-Bass.

Marken, S., Gray, L., & Lewis, L. (2013). *Dual enrollment programs and courses for high school students at postsecondary institutions: 2010–11* (NCES 2013-002). Washington, DC: National Center for Education Statistics, U.S. Department of Education. Retrieved from http://nces.ed.gov/pubs2013/2013002.pdf

McLaughlin, M. (1987). Learning from experience: Lessons from policy implementation. *Educational Evaluation and Policy Analysis, 9*(2), 171–178.

Ohio Board of Regents. (2010, August 25). *The Ohio articulation and transfer policy.* Retrieved from http://regents.ohio.gov/transfer/policy/CreditTransferPolicy.pdf

Pretlow, J., & Wathington, H. (2014). Expanding dual enrollment: Increasing postsecondary access for all? *Community College Review, 42*(1), 41–54.

Stone, D. (2012). *Policy paradox: The art of political decision making* (3rd ed.). New York, NY: WW Norton & Company.

Virginia Plan for Dual Enrollment (VPDE). (2008, March). *Virginia plan for dual enrollment between Virginia public schools and community colleges.* Retrieved from http://www.vccs.edu/wp-content/uploads/2013/07/signed-VA-plan-for-dual-enrollment-2008.pdf

Western Interstate Commission for Higher Education (WICHE). (2013). *Knocking at the college door: Projections of high school graduates—Ohio.* Retrieved from http://www.wiche.edu/info/knocking-8th/profiles/oh.pdf

JOSHUA PRETLOW is an assistant professor of community college leadership at Old Dominion University in Norfolk, VA.

JENNIFER PATTESON is a dual enrollment coordinator at Thomas Nelson Community College in Hampton, VA.

3

Policy, financial, and transportation barriers have limited participation in dual enrollment for marginalized (low-socioeconomic, first-generation, and ethnic minority) students in Oklahoma. This chapter presents a collaborative effort by education and community leaders that has successfully eliminated these barriers and increased the number of marginalized students participating in dual enrollment.

Eliminating Barriers to Dual Enrollment in Oklahoma

Rick Roach, Juanita Gamez Vargas, Kevin M. David

Program Development

In early 2010, the Tulsa P-20 Council, an action committee composed of over 20 community, nonprofit, and education leaders in Tulsa County, Oklahoma, examined the high dropout rates in the Tulsa Public School (TPS) district. The P-20 Council is a subcouncil of the Community Service Council of Tulsa, which is a Tulsa area United Way partner. The Tulsa Community College (TCC) president and the superintendents of TPS and Union Public School (UPS) districts had been meeting informally for breakfast to discuss educational needs in the Tulsa area and decided to present the idea to expand dual enrollment at the P-20 Council meetings. During the discussions, several superintendents for Tulsa area schools noted the positive impact that dual enrollment appeared to have on the performance and persistence of their students. Council members also identified several barriers to dual enrollment including policy barriers in the form of high academic admission standards, financial barriers in the form of substantial textbook and enrollment fees, and transportation barriers since dual enrollment opportunities were only available on college campuses. After identifying these barriers the council decided to develop a plan to eliminate the barriers and "Increase accessibility to higher education for all students including concurrent enrollment and dual enrollment programs" (Tulsa County P-20 Council, 2010, Objective 2). The purpose of this chapter is to describe these barriers

NEW DIRECTIONS FOR COMMUNITY COLLEGES, no. 169, Spring 2015 © 2015 Wiley Periodicals, Inc.
Published online in Wiley Online Library (wileyonlinelibrary.com) • DOI: 10.1002/cc.20130

and how Tulsa navigated and eliminated these barriers to increase access to dual enrollment for low-socioeconomic, first-generation, and ethnic minority students.

Public relations and marketing departments from TCC, UPS, and TPS collaborated to create marketing materials and coined the term "EXCELerate" to brand the pilot project and differentiate it from regular dual enrollment at TCC.

Addressing Policy Barriers.   The Oklahoma State Regents for Higher Education (OSRHE) is the governing body for higher education in the state of Oklahoma. The OSRHE supports dual enrollment by requiring that all high schools provide information to students about dual enrollment and offering 100% tuition waivers for high school seniors. Based on the philosophy that only upper-academic students could be successful, current admission policies favor upper-academic students (i.e., OSRHE policy of 21 ACT or 3.5 GPA for juniors and 19 ACT or 3.0 GPA for seniors). However, research indicates that mid-academic-level students also have the potential to be successful in dual enrollment courses (Karp, 2012). Thus, TCC submitted a request on behalf of the P-20 Council to the OSRHE to develop and implement a pilot project with TPS and UPS supporting a goal to eliminate barriers to dual enrollment, and the request included seven exceptions for the EXCELerate pilot project.

The first exception request addressed OSRHE's admission policy of 21 ACT or 3.5 GPA for juniors and 19 or 3.0 GPA for seniors. The exception for admitting dual enrollment students with a 19 ACT or 2.5 GPA was granted, with the rationale that it would allow mid-academic-level high school students attending TPS and UPS schools to participate in dual enrollment at TCC. The second exception request was related to OSRHE's policy that sophomores were not allowed to participate in dual enrollment. The exception allowed sophomores with a 19 ACT PLAN test score to enroll in TCC's Strategies for Academic Success, a study skills course. The ACT PLAN test is a predictor of ACT performance and is administered to all sophomore students in the state of Oklahoma. The proposal's rationale was that the course would prepare students for future dual enrollment courses. The third exception targeted OSRHE's policy that a high school student may not enroll in a combined number of high school and college credits above 19 semester credit hours. Because extracurricular courses are included in this calculation, students who are enrolled in sports, band, and other extracurricular courses face barriers to enrolling in dual enrollment courses. The exception allowed a combined college workload of 19 semester credit hours excluding extracurricular elective courses. The rationale for this exception was that students could incorporate extracurricular elective courses into their schedule and still be successful in college courses.

The fourth exception regarded OSRHE's policy that high school students must maintain a college cumulative GPA of 2.0. The exception request was to allow students who fall below 2.0 to be placed on academic probation for one semester to allow them the opportunity to continue enrollment and improve their performance. The fifth exception related to OSRHE's policy that high school teachers may not teach college courses at a high school during the day. The exception allowed high school teachers who meet TCC full-time faculty qualifications to teach dual enrollment courses at the high school. The rationale was that having qualified high school teachers who can teach TCC courses would promote collegiality between high school and college faculty and ensure financial sustainability of the program. The sixth exception was in response to OSRHE's policy that high school students are not allowed to enroll in any remedial courses offered by colleges or universities designed to remove basic academic skill deficiencies. The exception allows dually admitted students to enroll in remedial courses offered by TCC. The rationale was that TCC would provide remedial courses on the high school campus in collaboration with high school faculty to ensure that course content would prepare students for college-level work.

The seventh and final exception was to allow the ACT PLAN (otherwise known as PLAN) test score to be used as a qualifier for dual enrollment. The policy exception allowed a minimum PLAN composite test score of 19 (equivalent to an ACT composite score range of 20–24) to be used to admit juniors and seniors. The rationale for the policy exception was that the cost of the ACT exam is a barrier for low-income students, whereas the OSRHE pays for the PLAN. The PLAN is administered to all high school students in Oklahoma during their sophomore year and is a reliable predictor of performance on the regular ACT.

Addressing Financial Barriers.   Eighty-five percent of students at TPS and 62% of UPS students qualify for free and reduced lunch (i.e., low-income) and may not afford tuition, fees, and textbooks required to participate in dual enrollment. Approval of the policy exceptions and a financial agreement between TCC, TPS, and UPS created an unprecedented opportunity for students to enroll in dual enrollment college coursework at a high school campus during the regular school day for a greatly reduced price. This financial agreement provided full-time TCC faculty to be reassigned to act as EXCELerate faculty liaisons who provided oversight for part-time faculty and the high school classrooms (technology, space, classroom environment). The agreement also reduced TCC's course enrollment fees for EXCELerate students from approximately $100 to $12.75 per three-credit-hour course. In addition, the school districts agreed to purchase the college course textbooks. Since the textbooks were a significant investment by the public schools, the TCC faculty liaisons guaranteed a minimum two-year life cycle for courses taught at high schools so the high schools would not absorb the cost of new textbooks every academic year. The EXCELerate students checked out the textbooks, were

New Directions for Community Colleges • DOI: 10.1002/cc

allowed to take them home, and returned the textbooks at the end of the semester.

Addressing Transportation Barriers. Since many high school students depend on a district school bus for transportation to the high school, many students are unable to drive to TCC to participate in dual enrollment at the college. TCC agreed to offer courses at TPS and UPS high school locations during the EXCELerate pilot program with the provision that a collegiate environment and course rigor be maintained. By offering college courses at high school locations during the day, students without their own transportation could now participate in dual enrollment through EXCELerate.

Program Results

The TCC Planning and Institutional Research Department provided data analysis for five semesters during the EXCELerate pilot program (for more details about the methodology and analysis, see Gamez Vargas, Roach, & David, 2014). Student enrollment and success measures of EXCELerate students were compared as a cohort group to high school students who took TCC courses on one of TCC's four campuses during the same semesters. Analyses examined demographic as well as student success measures. Of particular interest regarding demographics, results from chi-square tests revealed that significantly more Black or African American (8.9% vs. 1.5%) and Hispanic (8.8% vs. 2.8%) students, as well as juniors (23.8% vs. 13.3%), were enrolled in the EXCELerate group than in the group of non-EXCELerate high schools students who took courses on TCC campuses.

Findings related to student success indicated that rates of enrollment in TCC courses in the next semester were comparable across the EXCELerate and on-campus dual enrollment student groups (see Table 3.1 for details). Subsequent enrollment numbers counted students multiple times if they

Table 3.1   Student Success Outcomes Across Five Semesters for EXCELerate and Non-EXCELerate Students

Outcome	EXCELerate (n = 1,118)	On-Campus Dual Enrollment (n = 1,794)
TCC enrollment in subsequent term	934 of 1,699 (55.0%)	1,440 of 2,624 (54.9%)
Matriculation to TCC next fall	264 of 863 seniors (30.6%)	387 of 1,347 seniors (28.7%)
Course retention (grades other than W)	2,143 of 2,336 (91.7%)	3,963 of 4,123 (96.1%)
Grades of C or better	1,945 of 2,336 (83.3%)	3,702 of 4,123 (89.8%)

Note: Forty-eight students took courses in the EXCELerate program as well as on one of TCC's campuses; these students are counted in both groups to most accurately reflect the student populations taking courses at the different locations.

NEW DIRECTIONS FOR COMMUNITY COLLEGES • DOI: 10.1002/cc

enrolled in multiple terms since the beginning of the EXCELerate program because they may have enrolled again after one semester but not another. Moreover, rates of fall matriculation to TCC for high school seniors enrolled in the previous spring semester were similar across the two groups. Chi-square tests indicated that dual enrolled students taking classes at TCC campuses had significantly higher rates of course retention (i.e., grades other than Withdrawal or Administrative Withdrawal) and grades of C or better than those in the EXCELerate group. Although further exploration would help elucidate the factors underlying these differences, EXCELerate students would be expected to have somewhat lower success rates in general because they began with lower GPAs and test scores. Yet, the success rates of both groups were higher than the overall rates for all TCC students, suggesting high levels of success for dual enrolled students both at their high schools and on TCC's campuses.

As a result of the pilot project, several notable developments have occurred. TCC developed an office of High School Relations and appointed a dean, who subsequently was endowed as a chair of Collegiate Academies by the George Kaiser Family Foundation. UPS completed a $28 million Union Collegiate Academy construction project, and TPS created the Will Rogers College High School during the "Project Schoolhouse" efficiency initiative in 2011–2012. TPS completed an extensive renovation to the Will Rogers College High School annex building at a cost of $850,000 in order to provide students an authentic collegiate experience. These developments indicate growing support in the Tulsa area for expanding college access to high school students through dual enrollment while maintaining course quality and supporting a collegiate experience.

Challenges and Solutions

Although the EXCELerate program has experienced many successes, implementation has not come without its challenges. For example, TCC faculty expressed legitimate concerns for maintaining college rigor and a collegiate experience on the high school campus. It also became apparent that some faculty felt threatened and saw the EXCELerate program as competition for enrollment at TCC campuses. The dean of High School Relations collaborated with the TCC Faculty Association Executive Board to create a Faculty Association Concurrent Enrollment (FACE) committee to address these concerns. Working together, the vice president for Academic Affairs, dean of High School Relations, and the FACE committee developed dual enrollment partnership guidelines based on the National Alliance of Concurrent Enrollment Partnerships (NACEP) standards. The committee also established a list of approved general education courses that could be offered at the high schools, choosing freshman-level courses that EXCELerate students were most likely to be successful in and benefit from as well as courses that were transferable to all Oklahoma public higher education institutions. The FACE committee and dean of High School Relations continue to meet monthly and collaborate on emerging issues. The faculty liaisons make classroom observations every semester and inspect classrooms for technology readiness and an environment conducive to a collegiate experience. The meetings are also important in an effort to continually improve EXCELerate program outcomes.

Another challenge related to how Oklahoma high schools awarded credit to dual enrollment students. Oklahoma Senate Bill 290 was enacted into law in July 2009 and mandated that dual enrolled students receive credit for both high school and college as a core course if the high school and community college curricula are aligned. For example, college Composition I and II classes have typically been considered by most high schools to have equivalent learning outcomes to high school senior English; however, college nutrition courses are transcripted back to high schools as physical education, science, biology, or sometimes as an elective. Almost five years later local school boards are still inconsistent in many areas such as awarding core or elective credit or if final grades will be weighted or nonweighted. EXCELerate has been an impetus for equity in this area as it expands to include more school districts. The trend has been to increase high school core credits from one half to one semester credit and to weight grades similarly to Advanced Placement (AP) scores. This is a significant shift in the academic landscape and will likely increase dual enrollment participation by students previously attracted to AP courses.

Future Considerations

The OSRHE implemented the tuition waiver reimbursement for up to six credit hours per semester to public colleges and universities in Oklahoma for high school senior students in 2005. While the tuition waiver has been helpful, the state has not been able to fully fund tuition waivers for high school senior students over the past several years. Although a majority of public higher education institutions in the state have continued to provide tuition waivers for high school senior students, TCC has continued to cover not only seniors but juniors as well with supplementary financial support from the TCC Foundation. The result is that TCC is now heavily subsidizing the cost for dual enrollment at $270,000 per semester. TCC is committed to supporting dual enrollment but the financial reality is that as participation increases the resulting increased cost could become a limitation to sustainability and growth. In early discussions about funding, participating high schools agreed to allow TCC to utilize their teachers with 15 graduate hours in the core course discipline to teach college courses at the high school during the day. Yet, a number of factors have affected the high school partners' abilities to implement the use of qualified high school teachers. For instance, one limitation is that since Oklahoma has not previously allowed high school teachers to teach college courses at the high school, teachers have not been motivated to complete graduate hours in core disciplines, opting instead to complete graduate hours in education while in pursuit of a master's degree in education. This results in an extremely limited pool of qualified high school teachers. The high schools have also been limited by budget cuts and cannot afford to reallocate teacher load from regular high school courses to college courses.

An additional research study has been commissioned to more fully understand perspectives of all stakeholders in the EXCELerate pilot program. The new study utilizes research instruments to collect qualitative data that will inform the development of a logic model. The logic model is an integral component of a long-term strategic plan and will help stakeholders make decisions to establish sustainability of the EXCELerate program.

Conclusion

The results of the data analysis are favorable for continuing the EXCELerate program and the model has already been expanded to other area high schools. College courses are offered at the high schools or at area community campuses (career tech centers, satellite and state university campuses in the TCC service area). The $12.75 three-credit-hour course fee has been renewed for an additional year at TPS and UPS but is $36.75 at new EXCELerate locations, reflecting the addition of the technology fee to the library and assessment fee. In addition, OSHRE has extended the pilot project for the academic year 2015–2016. These OSRHE policy exceptions remain limited to TPS and UPS until OSRHE determines if any policy exceptions should be considered for continuation, expansion, or implementation at the state level. The findings and implications of this report are significant because they address challenges of recruitment, retention, and ultimately the need to have an understanding of the experiences of marginalized students who are capable of, but not previously identified for, early college success. Moreover, by gathering data about marginalized students, institutions can more fully support these students' needs for early college success. Results of this study may be generalizable to larger populations of students who could benefit from similar strategies and interventions. The state of Oklahoma would benefit from policy revisions informed by data and information included in this chapter.

References

Gamez Vargas, J., Roach, R., & David, K. M. (2014). Successful concurrent programs: An EXCELerate program in OK. *Community College Journal of Research and Practice*, 38, 166–173.

Karp, M. M. (2012). "I don't know, I've never been to college!" Dual enrollment as a college readiness strategy. In E. Hofmann & D. Voloch (Eds.), *New Directions for Higher Education: No. 158. Dual enrollment: strategies, outcomes, and lessons for school–college partnerships* (pp. 21–28). San Francisco, CA: Jossey-Bass. doi:10.1002/he.20011

Tulsa County P-20 Council. (2010). *2010 Proposed Work Plan*. Retrieved from http://www.csctulsa.org/files/file/P-20%20Council%20work%20plan.doc

RICK ROACH *is the dean of High School Relations and George Kaiser Family Foundation Endowed Chair of Collegiate Academies at Tulsa Community College.*

JUANITA GAMEZ VARGAS *is assistant professor in the Educational Leadership & Policy Studies Department, Adult and Higher Education (EDAH) program at the University of Oklahoma.*

KEVIN M. DAVID *is the associate vice president for institutional effectiveness at Tulsa Community College.*

NEW DIRECTIONS FOR COMMUNITY COLLEGES • DOI: 10.1002/cc

4

Emerging early college models are providing opportunities for high school students to accrue college credits and experience themselves as successful college students. The states of Michigan and New York are at the forefront of state-level efforts to offer early college models to a wider range of high school students. This chapter features early college models and describes the variety of programmatic designs and student experiences.

Emerging Early College Models for Traditionally Underserved Students

Elisabeth Barnett, Evelyn Maclutsky, Chery Wagonlander

Engaging in dual enrollment courses has been found to improve educational outcomes for students, in particular low-income and minority students (An, 2013; Karp, Calcagno, Hughes, Jeong, & Bailey, 2007; Speroni, 2011). Participating students are more likely to graduate high school, enroll and persist in college, accrue college credits, and complete college than students who do not participate in dual enrollment. However, there are still many barriers to both participation and success. For the most part, students are only able to take dual enrollment courses if they meet the standard requirements to enter college-level work at the participating institution, most commonly by passing college placement tests (Barnett & Stamm, 2010). What is more, students do not have access to dual enrollment if enrolled in high schools with low or no involvement in dual enrollment (Pretlow & Wathington, 2014; Taylor & Lichtenberger, 2013), and there may be uneven information available to students and families about dual enrollment options (Zinth, 2014).

Early and middle college high schools (E-MCHSs) are explicitly designed to provide dual enrollment opportunities to students who may not have had access to college in the past. Targeted to students from groups traditionally underrepresented in college, they are structured to offer a suite of experiences and supports that lead to success in both high school and college courses. The "classic" E-MCHS is a small high school located on a college campus that offers a curriculum blending high school and college coursework. The school's small, personalized environment complements

New Directions for Community Colleges, no. 169, Spring 2015 © 2015 Wiley Periodicals, Inc.
Published online in Wiley Online Library (wileyonlinelibrary.com) • DOI: 10.1002/cc.20131

the collegiate surroundings, thereby encouraging students to tackle and succeed in college coursework. Students begin taking college classes as early as 9th grade at no cost to them or their parents, and many of the credits earned count toward high school graduation as well as toward a college degree. While middle college high schools offer an opportunity to take college classes, early college high schools create academic plans that allow students to earn at least a year's worth of college credit and even an associate's degree by the time they graduate high school. Because they are very similar, we refer to early and middle colleges as E-MCHSs in this chapter. An experimental evaluation of classic E-MCHSs found that participating students were considerably more likely than students in traditional high schools to graduate high school, enroll in college, and earn college degrees (Berger, Turk-Bicakci, Garet, Knudson, & Hoshen, 2014).

Although the number of these schools is growing, there are still only about 280 in the United States for a number of reasons (Jobs for the Future, 2014a). Colleges cannot accommodate unlimited numbers of high school students on their campuses, and not all students want to engage in a curriculum as challenging as that offered in the E-MCHS. By design, the schools are small, limiting the number of students who can attend. In addition, starting and sustaining an E-MCHS can be a challenging enterprise.

However, a number of schools and districts are conceptualizing and implementing models that offer supported dual enrollment in comprehensive high schools. Through programs sometimes called Early College Designs (Jobs for the Future, 2014b), Smart Scholars (Frey, 2011), or Enhanced Dual Enrollment Systems (Middle College National Consortium, 2014), students take selected college courses while in high school, with carefully structured supports used to facilitate their success. This experience is designed to allow a smooth transition to college attendance after graduation from high school. Models have been developed through local school–college partnerships as well as through state initiatives or sponsorship from intermediary organizations.

The states of Michigan and New York are at the forefront of state-level efforts to expand access to college-course-taking opportunities to a wider range of high school students based on the belief that this may encourage postsecondary enrollment and success. Although both states are using the national E-MCHS models as inspiration, each has allowed for the creation of a wide range of programmatic designs and student experiences. In Michigan, three early college design models are utilized: fifth year programs; enhanced dual enrollment system (EDES) programs; and science, technology, engineering, and math (STEM) early college programs. In New York, a number of programmatic variations have developed including Smart Scholars cohort programs within schools and P-TECH schools.

The participating high schools include many that serve low-income, urban, and rural communities with large numbers of students who would be the first in their family to attend college. It should be noted that despite the diversity of models, all are taking into account research-based design considerations (see Barnett, Bucceri, Hindo, & Kim, 2011) including: (a) attention to strong high school–college partnerships; (b) careful sequencing of courses and supports that allow students to progress toward greater independence; (c) built-in opportunities to gain college knowledge, that is, the knowledge needed to navigate formal and informal college systems; (d) measures to ensure the authenticity of college courses; and (e) a focus on key relationships that help students to believe that they can succeed in challenging college courses.

The purpose of this chapter is to provide examples of new early college models in Michigan and New York that expand underserved students' access to dual enrollment and provide a pathway to college. All involve high schools and colleges working together to create blended educational approaches. These new models are of particular interest because they offer images of evidence-based innovative ways to improve college access and success upon which others can build.

The Michigan Experience

Like many other states, Michigan has rates of high school graduation and college enrollment that are not sufficient to meet its educational and economic development goals. In 2009, the high school graduation rate was 71%, and, in 2010, the percent of students entering college after high school graduation was 62% (NCHEMS, 2014). These figures are below the national average of an 80% high school graduation rate (Stetser & Stillwell, 2014) and 66% of high school students who transition to college immediately after high school graduation (U.S. Department of Education, National Center for Education Statistics, 2013). In addition, the achievement gap among students in Michigan in terms of college readiness is considered among the widest in the country (Education Trust, 2012). A major motivation for expanding access to dual enrollment in Michigan comes from concerns about these data.

Emerging Models in Michigan.   Currently, in the state of Michigan, there are more than 58 high school dual enrollment providers including stand-alone schools, charters, academies, schools within a school, and district programs. In the 2012–2013 school year, there were 72,718 college course enrollments by Michigan high school students compared to 13,952 in the 2001–2002 school year (B. Barber, Michigan Department of Education, personal communication, 2014). This growth was led and supported by various state governmental and educational policies, as well as by leadership from the Office of Career and Technical Education at the Michigan Department of Education, the Michigan Early Middle College Association, and the Mott Foundation. In addition, the state enacted changes in graduation requirements and policy reforms that supported the growth of dual enrollment and early college designs.

NEW DIRECTIONS FOR COMMUNITY COLLEGES • DOI: 10.1002/cc

The Michigan E-MCHS reform movement began in 1991 with the opening of Mott Middle College High School (MMCHS) on the campus of Mott Community College in Flint, Michigan. This unique K–12/college partnership was designed to lower dropout rates and expand college enrollment and completion among high-potential, at-risk youth. MMCHS challenged prevailing beliefs about what at-risk youth could accomplish. They demonstrated that it was possible to create a positive and nurturing high school environment that fosters academic success in a higher education setting. Drawing on the experiences and principles of the Middle College National Consortium, MMCHS quickly became a model site for outreach, replication, and research of middle college concepts and models in Michigan and nationally.

In the 2002–2003 school year, MMCHS began its redesign into an E-MCHS in concert with the growing national Early College High School Initiative, supported by the Bill and Melinda Gates Foundation. The redesign involved a purposeful integration of dual enrollment courses with the courses included in the Michigan Merit Curriculum, specifically those required for high school graduation in the state. Since that time, MMCHS has offered students a wider range of dual enrollment courses, and the 2013 MMCHS graduating class left high school with an average of 30 college credits earned (NCREST, 2014).

Recognizing this success, in 2006, Governor Granholm redirected discretionary funds to establish a $2 million annual line item to support the start-up of new E-MCHSs. At the same time, the Mott Foundation allocated funds to support a partnership for technical assistance between Mott Community College and the Michigan Department of Education. These two actions, buoyed by a positive policy environment, resulted in the successful opening of eight Allied Health E-MCHSs by the 2009–2010 school year. This new wave sparked the creation and formalization of the Michigan Early-Middle College Association (MEMCA) as a forum for ongoing peer-to-peer coaching. Currently, more than 50 E-MCHSs, early college programs, and enhanced dual enrollment systems—in varying stages of development—meet under the MEMCA umbrella.

E-MCHS Models in Michigan. While the number of classic (full school) E-MCHSs continues to expand—there are 17 in the state as of 2014—a variety of other models have emerged in Michigan based on E-MCHS principles. Three models are especially noteworthy: (a) fifth year programs, (b) enhanced dual enrollment systems, and (c) the STEM Early College Expansion Project (SECEP) schools.

Fifth Year Programs. E-MCHS fifth year programs are embedded within comprehensive high schools. They allow participating students to earn a high school diploma and a substantial number of college credits by graduating high school in five years instead of four. Schools and districts developing fifth year programs enter into a formal agreement with one or more postsecondary partners and must obtain authorization from the Michigan

Department of Education. Students in these programs have the opportunity to take free college courses while still receiving support from their home high school. Fifth year programs are of particular value for students who might not attend or succeed in college without a thoughtfully supported transition. School districts receive full funding for each participating student, a portion of which is distributed to the college to cover the cost of tuition.

Students must be appropriately flagged as participants in the program and placed in a five-year graduation cohort for state/school accountability purposes. Students in their fifth year must not yet be eligible for graduation and must take at least one high school course in addition to their college courses, which typically count for dual credit. College courses are taken on campus, online, or in cohorted sections at the home high school. According to the Michigan Department of Education, 17 high schools offer fifth year programs in the state of Michigan with about 3,700 students enrolled in the 2013–2014 academic year (B. Barber, personal communication, 2014).

While fifth year programs are likely to benefit many students, some questions have been raised about the trade-offs involved. For example, participants will have less time as independent college students, possibly limiting opportunities for personal growth, exploration of different majors and career directions, and participation in extracurricular activities. In addition, students may struggle in their college courses during the fifth year program, resulting in a less than ideal transcript and limiting opportunities for transfer and financial aid. Finally, students may not experience all of the important high school milestones with their high school class. Overall, however, we believe that evaluations will show that the benefits outweigh the costs.

Enhanced Dual Enrollment Systems.   To offer more students the chance to take college courses, some Michigan school districts have established enhanced dual enrollment systems (EDES). Under this model, students who may not be ready to tackle dual enrollment independently are provided with supports that promote their success in college courses. EDES models vary but all are guided by a goal of "12×12" whereby students work to earn 12 college course credits by the end of their 12th grade year. Based on practices developed in E-MCHS, EDES programs are based on strong K–12/higher education partnerships and incorporate: (a) early assessment with guidance to ensure that students are provided the assistance that they need to prepare to take college courses; (b) sequenced, selected dual enrollment courses linked to the students' academic plan; (c) support for college courses in the form of companion courses in the subject area or tutoring; (d) early warning systems that alert the high school when a student is struggling in college courses and allow for timely intervention; and (e) shared data collection and use to make sure that the program is on course. As of 2014, 27 high schools offer enhanced dual enrollment with approximately 1,300 students participating.

NEW DIRECTIONS FOR COMMUNITY COLLEGES • DOI: 10.1002/cc

STEM Early College Expansion Project (SECEP) Schools.   In January 2014, several Michigan independent school districts were awarded a US-DOE Investing in Innovation (I3) grant to replicate the early college high school model and also improve STEM education. The other organizations involved are the Michigan Early Middle College Association; the Middle College National Consortium; Jobs for the Future; and the National Center for Restructuring Education, Schools and Teaching at Teachers College, Columbia University.

Eleven high schools are working with colleges to structure pathways into STEM college majors and to help teachers improve their knowledge and skills related to teaching STEM subjects. Participating students will engage in the kinds of experiences and supports typically offered in an E-MCHS, including the chance to earn 12 or more college credits. In addition to improving STEM education overall, the project proposes to decrease dropout rates and boost college enrollment among underrepresented populations.

The New York Experience

Similar to Michigan, New York has a persistent achievement gap. In 2013, the statewide graduation rate for New York public school students who entered 9th grade in 2009 was 74.9% (New York State Education Department, 2014), below the national average of 80% (Stetser & Stillwell, 2014); underlying this figure at the state level was almost a 30 percentage point gap between the graduation rates of White students compared to Hispanic or African American students. The gap for students with disabilities (SWDs) and English language learners (ELLs) compared to the statewide rate was even greater: almost 30 percentage points for SWDs and over 40 percentage points for ELLs (New York State Education Department, 2014).

The state of New York is committed to the idea that dual enrollment and early college can help address the achievement gap and has a long history with this approach. In 1972, the state's first dual enrollment program was initiated at Syracuse University and called Project Advance, a dual enrollment program in which college courses are taught by qualified high school teachers on the high school campus. In 2014, Project Advance offered 38 courses to 9,400 students in 184 high schools in five states and three continents. Another major dual enrollment program in New York State is the City University of New York's (CUNY) College Now program, initiated in 1983, that includes all 18 CUNY two-year and four-year colleges and over 400 New York City high schools; it serves 20,000 students annually.

The first E-MCHSs in the country are located in New York State and they have served as the models for all of the E-MCHSs that have followed. In 1974, the first Middle College High School opened on the campus of LaGuardia Community College, a CUNY college. In 2001, in partnership with the New York City Department of Education, Bard College opened its first High School Early College in Manhattan. In 2002, CUNY launched the

Early College Initiative (ECI) to redesign existing MCHSs and develop new schools as Early College High Schools (ECHSs). The CUNY ECI now has 17 schools in partnership with the New York City Department of Education, seven of which include middle school as well as high school grades.

Emerging Models in New York. Building on this rich history, the New York State Board of Regents launched the Smart Scholars ECHS program in 2009 to help address the state's achievement gap. A combination of private and state funding supported the implementation of 23 Smart Scholars ECHS programs across the state. Whereas the original ECHS model included only stand-alone high schools, the Smart Scholars program funded both early college high schools and early college programs within schools in an effort to scale and adapt the model to a broader range of settings.

The Smart Scholars' goal is to provide students the opportunity and support to earn at least 24 and up to 60 college credits prior to high school graduation. None of the Smart Scholars schools or programs is located on a college campus, and their proximity to the partner college campus varies. All schools and programs include student supports as well as activities that bring students onto the partner college's campus to strengthen the students' identity as future college students. There are seven stand-alone schools in the Smart Scholars network and 16 programs within schools.

Similar to many other E-MCHSs, the Smart Scholars schools and programs had the support of an intermediary organization during their initial four years of planning and implementation that helped ensure alignment with key early college design principles. The intermediary for the Smart Scholars program was SUNY/EDWorks, a partnership between SUNY's Office of the Education Pipeline and EDWorks, a national nonprofit based in Ohio that provides technical assistance to help public schools improve student achievement and access to postsecondary education.

A recent evaluation of the Smart Scholars ECHS program conducted by the National Center for Restructuring Education, Schools and Teaching at Teachers College, Columbia University, found that the average number of college courses offered in 2011–2012 was 8.8 for the schools and programs that opened in 2010 and 6.5 for those that opened in 2011 (Barnett, Kim, Zander, & Avilo, 2013). Eighty-three percent of the students earned a grade of "C" or higher in their college courses, while 92% passed with a grade of "D" or higher. The researchers praised the Smart Scholars program for its effectiveness in enrolling the target population (e.g., 71% were eligible for the free or reduced price lunch program, 84% were racial/ethnic minorities, and 51% were male), serving large numbers of students (over 4,800 in 2012–2013), high-quality implementation of whole-school and cohort-model programs, strong partnerships with postsecondary institutions, high college course enrollment and passing rates, evidence of authentic college courses being offered, and strong leadership by the state and intermediary.

In New York State, as in Michigan, a number of different models have evolved to address different needs and conditions. These include the

Smart Scholars cohort models within comprehensive high schools and the P-TECH schools.

Cohort Models.   Ten of the 23 Smart Scholars grantees are cohort models, generally serving 25–50 students per grade level. Five are academies located in a distinct section of a school building with a dedicated teaching staff and principal or lead teacher. The rest are striving to approach this model by coordinating the students' class schedules and identifying a team of teachers who will instruct as many of the students' core high school courses as possible. All programs provide an array of support services to prepare the students for college-level work and support them when taking college courses via advisories, mentoring, tutoring, seminars, and test prep classes, for example. College courses are usually taught by qualified high school teachers; however, some programs move students to the college campus for courses during their junior and senior years for full or half days. In a few programs, all college courses are taught by college faculty.

In an effort to provide students with college campus experiences, the programs have developed a variety of special features and innovations. Most of the programs offer a campus-based summer program for incoming 9th grade students and returning students. For example, Schenectady County Community College's program with Schenectady High School provides incoming 9th grade students with a summer course entitled Freshmen Success Seminar for which students can earn one college credit. The course focuses on goal setting, time management skills, and team building. The companion noncredit course is called Literacy for Social Action and focuses on improving reading and writing skills through a service learning curriculum.

Another example is SUNY Old Westbury's partnership with Roosevelt High School that developed a program called Fridays on Campus that provides weekly lab classes on the SUNY Old Westbury campus to students taking college math and science classes at the high school. SUNY Old Westbury faculty and lab instructors partner with the qualified high school teachers to provide these classes. In addition to the academic experiences, students get the chance to experience life as a college student; for example, they often eat lunch on the college campus on the days they have classes there.

NYS P-TECH Schools and Program.   In fall 2011, the Pathways in Technology Early College High School (P-TECH) opened its doors in New York City. Governed by CUNY, the New York City Department of Education, and IBM, P-TECH represents a new version of the E-MCHS model. This model addresses career readiness as well as college readiness by a partnership among an employer, high school, and college. While most E-MCHSs are four- or five-year schools and programs, the P-TECH model includes a sixth year to allow time for every student to complete an associate's degree in a field aligned with the work of the employer partner and to integrate a workplace learning curriculum that includes setting individual career goals, project-based learning, guest speakers, mentoring, workplace visits, and internship experiences. IBM, the employer partner, has contributed

NEW DIRECTIONS FOR COMMUNITY COLLEGES • DOI: 10.1002/cc

significantly to the planning as well as implementation of the school's curriculum and will give the school's students priority consideration for employment when they graduate. Students can graduate with an Associate of Applied Science in Computer Information Systems or Electromechanical Engineering Technology by the end of their sixth year. Similar to Michigan's fifth year programs, the New York State accountability system allows for a sixth year graduation cohort and these students continue to generate state aid for their districts during all six years of enrollment.

New York Governor Andrew Cuomo has identified in the P-TECH model a strategy to address the academic achievement gap and also stimulate the state's economy. In 2013, he announced the New York State Pathways in Technology Early College High School (NYS P-TECH) program, modeled after the original P-TECH. Sixteen NYS P-TECH projects opened as schools or programs in each of New York's ten economic regions in the fall of 2014. The projects will serve over 800 9th grade students with a plan to add a new 9th grade class each year. In 2014, the state awarded funding to a second cohort of 10 NYS P-TECHs that will open in the fall of 2015, and the P-TECH model is being replicated in other parts of the country (Forrohar, 2014). Whereas the original P-TECH has one employer partner, several of the NYS P-TECH partnerships include multiple employer partners, from a range of businesses and industries, such as advanced manufacturing, architecture, and healthcare.

Final Thoughts

What does this array of different models mean for the future of dual enrollment? Most importantly, the models are all intended to offer students collegiate experiences while still in high school so that the transition to college can be as smooth and effective as possible. In some ways, these models have an important advantage over traditional dual enrollment; they also have advantages over "classic" E-MCHS. Traditional dual enrollment works primarily for students who are well prepared—academically and personally—to undertake challenging courses with very little support. It generally does not serve students who are struggling or in the academic middle; sometimes it serves them poorly, providing too little support for them to achieve success (Barnett & Stamm, 2010). Because they offer academic and social supports, the Michigan and New York models make participation in dual enrollment a possibility for a wider range of students, including those who may need bolstering along the way.

Most of the models discussed also have an advantage over regular E-MCHSs in that they are embedded in a regular school environment and are largely funded using existing revenue streams once established. They do not necessarily require space allocation at a college, separate administration and teachers, or a separate legal status. What is more, they make dual enrollment opportunities available to students who were not prepared in 9th grade to opt into a very different school model and challenging academic program.

In addition, some of the models discussed here allow for students with a career focus to pursue postsecondary studies that are well aligned with available jobs. They challenge the traditional division between career-technical or vocational education and academically focused education as students are engaging in rigorous college coursework while also preparing for careers. Through partnerships with business and industry as well as postsecondary institutions, they provide pathways to both college and career opportunities.

In sum, new types of dual enrollment in the form of E-MCHS models have the potential to increase opportunities for a wider range of students to start postsecondary studies early and achieve success in college and life. Partnering high school and college leaders are encouraged to look at the diverse models that currently exist and consider their fit with local priorities and environments. These, and new approaches that may yet emerge, have the potential to reduce time to degree, improve student opportunities, and provide cost-effective paths to higher education and employment.

References

An, B. P. (2013). The impact of dual enrollment on college degree attainment: Do low-SES students benefit? *Educational Evaluation and Policy Analysis, 35*(1), 57–75.

Barnett, E., Bucceri, K., Hindo, C., & Kim, J. (2011). *Ten key decisions in creating early colleges: Design options based on research.* New York, NY: National Center for Restructuring Education, Schools and Teaching (NCREST), Teachers College, Columbia University.

Barnett, E., Kim, J., Zander, S., & Avilo, O. (2013). *Smart Scholars early college high school program: Evaluation report.* Prepared for the University of the State of New York—Regents Research Fund. New York, NY: National Center for Restructuring Education, Schools and Teaching (NCREST), Teachers College, Columbia University.

Barnett, E., & Stamm, L. (2010). *Dual enrollment: A strategy for educational advancement of all students.* Washington, DC: Blackboard Institute.

Berger, A., Turk-Bicakci, L., Garet, M., Knudson, J., & Hoshen, G. (2014). *Early college, continued success: Early college high school initiative impact study.* Washington, DC: American Institutes for Research. Retrieved from http://www.air.org/files/AIR_ECHSI _Impact_Study_Report-_NSC_Update_01-14-14.pdf

Education Trust. (2012). *2012 MME and ACT college readiness results.* Retrieved from http://www.edtrust.org/sites/edtrust.org/files/publications/files/2013%20MME%20 and%20ACT%20College%20Readiness%20Results.pdf

Forrohar, R. (2014). The school that will get you a job. *TIME, 183*(7), 22–28.

Frey, J. P. (2011). *The Smart Scholars early college high school program—Cohort 2* [Information and RFP Webinar PowerPoint]. Retrieved from http://www.highered .nysed.gov/ss/rfp

Jobs for the Future. (2014a). *Reinventing high school for postsecondary success.* Retrieved from http://www.jff.org/initiatives/early-college-designs#.UziMO9x29go

Jobs for the Future. (2014b). *Early college designs: Overview and FAQ.* Retrieved from http://www.earlycolleges.org/overview.html#echs

Karp, M. M., Calcagno, J. C., Hughes, K. L., Jeong, D. W., & Bailey, T. R. (2007). *The postsecondary achievement of participants in dual enrollment: An analysis of student outcomes in two states.* New York, NY: Community College Research Center, Columbia University.

Middle College National Consortium. (2014). *Enhanced dual enrollment systems.* Retrieved from http://www.mcnc.us/enhanced-dual-enrollment-system/#sthash.fOzyneJf.dpbs

National Center for Higher Education Management Statistics (NCHEMS). (2014). *NCHEMS information center state profile report.* Retrieved from http://www.higheredinfo.org/stateprofile

National Center for Restructuring Education, Schools and Teaching (NCREST). (2014). *College access and success report, 2012–13: Mott Middle College.* New York, NY: Author.

New York State Education Department. (2014). *Graduation data—June 23, 2014.* Retrieved from http://www.p12.nysed.gov/irs/pressRelease/20140623/home.html

Pretlow, J., & Wathington, H. (2014). Expanding dual enrollment: Increasing postsecondary access for all? *Community College Review, 42*(1), 41–54.

Speroni, C. (2011). *Determinants of students' success: The role of advanced placement and dual enrollment programs* (NCPR Working Paper). New York, NY: National Center for Postsecondary Research.

Stetser, M., & Stillwell, R. (2014). *Public high school four-year on-time graduation rates and event dropout rates: School years 2010–11 and 2011–12.* First Look (NCES 2014-391). Washington, DC: National Center for Education Statistics, U.S. Department of Education. Retrieved from http://nces.ed.gov/pubs2014/2014391.pdf

Taylor, J. L., & Lichtenberger, E. J. (2013). *Who has access to dual credit in Illinois? Examining high school characteristics and dual credit participation rates* (IERC 2013-4). Edwardsville, IL: Illinois Education Research Council at Southern Illinois University Edwardsville.

U.S. Department of Education, National Center for Education Statistics. (2013). Table 302.10: Recent high school completers and their enrollment in 2-year and 4-year colleges, by sex: 1960 through 2012. In U.S. Department of Education, National Center for Education Statistics (Ed.), *Digest of education statistics* (2013 ed.). Retrieved from http://nces.ed.gov/programs/digest/d13/tables/dt13_302.10.asp

Zinth, J. D. (2014). *Increasing student access and success in dual enrollment programs: 13 model state-level policy components* (Report). Denver, CO: Education Commission of the States.

ELISABETH BARNETT *is a senior research associate at the Community College Research Center and associate director of the National Center for Restructuring Education, Schools and Teaching at Teachers College, Columbia University.*

EVELYN MACLUTSKY *is a project coordinator for the Office of Postsecondary Access, Support and Success at the New York State Education Department.*

CHERY WAGONLANDER *is the director of the Michigan Early/Middle College Association.*

5

Career and technical education concurrent enrollment may pose unique challenges in programming and enrollment for program administrators, and this chapter describes the experiences and challenges of a CTE concurrent enrollment administrator.

The Challenges of Career and Technical Education Concurrent Enrollment: An Administrative Perspective

Patricia W. Haag

When I first began working in career and technical education (CTE) concurrent enrollment in Maine, I knew very little about secondary or postsecondary CTE. At a community college in New York, I had overseen an academic concurrent enrollment partnership (CEP) that offered general education classes in English, humanities, math, science, and social sciences. I had also actively participated in the National Alliance of Concurrent Enrollment Partnerships (NACEP) from its first year, served on the NACEP Board of Directors for five years, and acquired NACEP accreditation for the program I oversaw. But none of these professional experiences prepared me for a new position developing a CTE concurrent enrollment partnership. The purpose of this chapter is to describe my experience as a new administrator of a CTE concurrent enrollment partnership at a community college in the Northeast. My intention is to describe the experiences and challenges I encountered as well as the lessons I learned as a new CTE concurrent enrollment administrator so that my experiences may be useful and valuable to CTE concurrent enrollment partnerships in other community college districts.

Program Background and Context

When I accepted the part-time concurrent enrollment consultant position at Southern Maine Community College (SMCC) in 2009, SMCC did not have a concurrent enrollment program. I was hired on the understanding that SMCC would soon offer concurrent enrollment classes to remain

New Directions for Community Colleges, no. 169, Spring 2015 © 2015 Wiley Periodicals, Inc.
Published online in Wiley Online Library (wileyonlinelibrary.com) • DOI: 10.1002/cc.20132

competitive with other community colleges in the state and to follow the national trend of replacing or supplementing Tech Prep articulation agreements with concurrent enrollment (Zinth, 2014). My original responsibility was to maintain and expand CTE escrow articulation agreements to fulfill the requirements of the state Perkins plan that 50% of colleges' technical programs be articulated with secondary CTE centers by 2013.

Within my first year at SMCC, the department chairs of Automotive Technology and Integrated Manufacturing Technology asked to offer concurrent enrollment classes in secondary CTE centers the following year. Their secondary CTE colleagues had persistently asked them to provide the same concurrent enrollment opportunities that several other community colleges provided. These two chairs were highly motivated to keep their programs competitive, and they believed that concurrent enrollment could be an effective recruitment tool, so they offered concurrent enrollment classes in academic year 2010–2011 as a pilot. Further, the chairs of the Early Childhood Education and Architectural and Engineering Design programs approved secondary CTE instructors who were teaching on the college campus part-time to offer concurrent enrollment classes at their secondary CTE centers. In this first academic year, 2010–2011, 68 CTE students enrolled in 12 sections of eight different CTE concurrent enrollment classes from four SMCC programs at six CTE centers.

Funding: Perkins, State, and College. SMCC relied primarily on funding from the federal Carl D. Perkins Career and Technical Education Act of 2006 to fund the administration of concurrent enrollment classes: one full-time director of School–College Partnerships, a position which was eliminated in fall 2012, and one part-time position which I held from fall 2009 to spring 2014. Because Perkins legislation is narrowly interpreted in Maine to fund technical education in CTE schools only, until spring 2013, the SMCC program focused exclusively on technical concurrent enrollment classes in secondary CTE centers taught during the school day by secondary CTE instructors approved by the college. The only other funding source was the Maine Community College System's (MCCS) On Course for College program, which reimburses community colleges for 50% of a limited number of concurrent enrollment students' tuition and requires that the college waive the other 50%. SMCC did not budget for any other program expenses such as supplies, events, or professional development.

Despite limited funding streams, there was reason to proceed confidently and optimistically. Based on data from Florida and New York (Karp, Calcagno, Hughes, Jeong, & Bailey, 2007), I knew that outcomes for students in CTE concurrent enrollment were comparable to outcomes for concurrent enrollment students in academic programs. Choosing to follow the NACEP standards as closely as possible, the college could ensure that any concurrent enrollment class was the equivalent of a course on the college campus.

NEW DIRECTIONS FOR COMMUNITY COLLEGES • DOI: 10.1002/cc

History and Evolution of CTE Concurrent Enrollment. When I began my position at SMCC, I was unaware that most of the unexpected challenges I faced with a new CTE concurrent enrollment program stemmed from the history and evolution of secondary CTE. The emphasis on college readiness in secondary CTE is fairly recent (ACTE, 2007). CTE programs, formerly known as vocational education, were historically separated from academic coursework (Stipanovic, Lewis, & Stringfield, 2012); qualifications required for secondary CTE instructors were different from those required for secondary instructors of academic subjects (National Research Center for Career and Technical Education [NRCCTE], 2010), and CTE students were generally more diverse than non-CTE students (NRCCTE, 2010). Perkins legislation began to address the increasing need to prepare CTE students for college with Tech Prep in 1990 in Perkins II, relying primarily on articulation agreements between secondary and postsecondary technical programs, and with programs of study that may include concurrent enrollment in 2006 with Perkins IV.

Challenges Specific to Career and Technical Education

Although current Perkins legislation and CTE professional organizations now embrace the need to prepare CTE students for college, elements of the earlier emphasis on workforce preparation for students who were not college bound remained embedded in the culture of many secondary CTE centers. These vestiges of the earlier secondary vocational education have, in my experience, presented challenges in programming, enrollment, and limited incentives in the development of a new CTE concurrent enrollment program. Furthermore, because CTE concurrent enrollment is a relatively recent development (Zinth, 2013), there are few descriptions of program elements necessary to address these difficulties, and states and colleges have had little guidance specific to CTE concurrent enrollment until recently.

Programming Difficulties. My first challenge in CTE concurrent enrollment was the difficulty of providing more than one or two introductory-level technical courses in any CTE program. Secondary CTE programs in Maine are not designed like college CTE programs: they are not divided into courses and there is no menu of courses from which to choose to fulfill program requirements. For example, Print Reading, a class housed in the college's Architectural and Engineering Design program, is a requirement in the college's Heating, Air Conditioning, and Refrigeration program, but high school CTE students in Heating, Air Conditioning, and Refrigeration programs at secondary CTE centers cannot take concurrent enrollment Print Reading when it is offered in the Drafting program at their CTE center because the CTE program does not allow them to take classes in other CTE programs. Secondary CTE instructors and administrators generally believe that the demands of meeting requirements for work-related certifications and industry-based standards in their programs are so great that they cannot afford to give their students time away for courses in other programs.

The persistent separation of academic and technical courses is another factor that limits the number and kind of college credits CTE students can earn through concurrent enrollment. Academic content is not formally, consistently integrated into technical courses across the state, so high schools do not consistently award credit for a secondary or concurrent enrollment English, math, or science class for completion of a technical program. Therefore, most secondary CTE students must complete their academic course requirements at their high schools. Stipanovic et al. (2012) noted that the majority of CTE centers nationally are still separate from high schools, so to earn college credit for academic courses such as English, math, and science, the majority of secondary CTE students either have to travel to a college campus or take academic concurrent enrollment classes at their high schools. Distances, transportation difficulties, scheduling conflicts, fear of the unknown, and uncertain plans about college often prevent CTE students from taking classes on college campuses, and time spent traveling between the high school and CTE center may prevent them from scheduling academic concurrent enrollment classes at their high school.

Low Enrollment.   Another difficulty I encountered with CTE concurrent enrollment was low enrollment numbers. CTE concurrent enrollment instructors were advising students not to take SMCC college classes if they did not want to attend SMCC because instructors knew that within the MCCS, introductory college courses in technical programs did not always transfer. Each semester, therefore, at least two or three CTE concurrent enrollment instructors, especially those outside the college's service area, would report that they "didn't have any students" for their class or had only a couple who wanted to attend SMCC. Some classes ran with only one or two students registered for college credit. Although I have had many conversations with instructors about the benefits of students taking free college classes regardless of transferability, CTE instructors persist with the notion that students should not register if they are not certain they will attend SMCC. Others do not believe that college is a good option for all CTE students.

Students also bring their own limitations, often the usual difficulties associated with first-generation college students. When I visited CTE concurrent enrollment classes for information or registration sessions, I was often surprised at how few secondary CTE students planned to attend college or understood the benefits of a college education. When secondary CTE students are interested in registering for concurrent enrollment classes, they often do not meet the placement test or SAT scores necessary to qualify. Again, I learned in hindsight that Levesque and Hudson (as cited in Bishop-Clark et al., 2010) found that students in CTE programs are generally less academically prepared, more diverse, and more likely to have special needs than non-CTE students in high schools (NRCCTE, 2010).

Although enrollment was not at all what I had hoped it would be in the first year, the matriculation rate of the 2010–2011 cohort was 36.5%; that is, 19 of 52 high school seniors who participated in CTE concurrent enrollment matriculated to SMCC the fall after their high school graduation. Given this early success for the first cohort, my supervisor recommended that the program be expanded.

Limited Incentives.   Determining how to expand the CTE concurrent enrollment program was bewildering. State funding did not provide strong incentives to the college administration. Maine's state appropriations to public colleges are not based on a Full-Time Equivalent (FTE) formula, so increases in enrollment from concurrent enrollment do not result in increased state funding to colleges. Although the MCCS On Course for College program reimburses community colleges 50% of concurrent enrollment students' tuition, colleges are required to waive the other 50%. Furthermore, the On Course for College funding awarded to each college is capped annually, and no additional program expenses such as administration, transportation, or professional development are covered by On Course for College.

Perkins also did not provide a strong policy incentive to the college. By 2011–2012, SMCC reached the state Perkins' requirement of articulating 50% of its technical programs with secondary CTE centers through traditional escrow articulation agreements alone. Escrow articulation agreements are a practice permitted by Perkins even though they are ineffective because students seldom use credits in escrow (Stipanovic et al., 2012), and credits in escrow are generally not transferable (Zinth, 2014). Perkins does not require concurrent enrollment, and student enrollment at SMCC was booming, so the college administration and most department chairs saw little need to dedicate scarce dollars to a program that was not required and not needed to boost enrollment. Recruiting new technical department chairs to support CTE concurrent enrollment expansion was difficult because they were already working harder than ever and had no short-term incentive to add to their already enormous workloads. Although student enrollment at SMCC increased 82% from fall 2004 to fall 2011 (from 4,103 to 7,482), the number of full-time faculty positions in that same time increased only 15.78%, and state appropriations to the college increased only 21.78%.

Relying on limited tuition reimbursements to the college from MCCS and on Perkins dollars caused the college's CTE-only concurrent enrollment program to stall. That is, state policy and federal Perkins policies did not provide the incentives needed to grow the program. The size and funding of the program changed little through the next three years except when enrollment fell to 36 in the third year, 2012–2013; changes were obviously needed.

New Directions for Community Colleges • DOI: 10.1002/cc

Recommendations

In 2013, SMCC began to explore high schools' interest in academic con-current enrollment courses, apparently motivated by slowing enrollment numbers on campus and the information that other MCCS community colleges were seeing significant matriculation rates from academic concurrent enrollment. A small increase in my salary from non-Perkins college operating funds freed me to work on developing academic concurrent enrollment classes in addition to CTE. The first academic class, US History, was offered at a high school in spring 2014. Concurrent enrollment course offerings and enrollment increased significantly in 2013–2014, and projections show an increase for 2014–2015. SMCC's decision to replace most traditional escrow articulation agreements with CTE concurrent enrollment in 2013–2014 also motivated more secondary CTE centers to offer concurrent enrollment classes.

Developing CTE concurrent enrollment programs is incredibly important and worthwhile, but academic concurrent enrollment courses may help provide momentum for CTE concurrent enrollment until there are greater incentives and support for CTE concurrent enrollment and until college readiness for all is truly integrated into secondary CTE. If colleges intend to rely on Perkins dollars and limited state funds to focus on CTE concurrent enrollment exclusively, the following recommendations may help address programming and enrollment challenges and create stronger incentives.

Initial Planning and Educating. Some state Perkins plans prohibit funding of separate academic concurrent enrollment classes that would help prepare CTE students for technical concurrent enrollment and enhance their college readiness, and many states are not providing sufficient support for either academic or CTE concurrent enrollment. Therefore, colleges that want to offer CTE concurrent enrollment need to understand the long-term financial benefits of concurrent enrollment: savings that result from documented increases in college enrollment, retention, and completion. Community colleges should study whether CTE concurrent enrollment students who matriculate at comparable colleges require less remediation, ask that other programs or organizations continue to study the effects of CTE concurrent enrollment on college remediation, and find people or organizations who can help calculate solid estimates of anticipated long-term revenues and savings.

Furthermore, community college administrators responsible for CTE concurrent enrollment should provide opportunities for faculty and staff to learn about the recruitment, retention, and college readiness agenda unique to concurrent enrollment and share research related to cost savings and revenue generating with faculty and staff. Ideally, administrators who understand the recruitment and retention agenda would insist on advanced planning that includes CTE concurrent enrollment goals in the college's strategic plan. Concurrent enrollment administrators could also provide incentives

NEW DIRECTIONS FOR COMMUNITY COLLEGES • DOI: 10.1002/cc

to department chairs by demonstrating to them that the work of concurrent enrollment is integral to the work of most offices on campus and does not fall on their shoulders alone.

Addressing CTE Programming and Enrollment Challenges. College administrators responsible for CTE concurrent enrollment also need to ask directors of secondary CTE centers about the academic standing or test scores of current CTE students in programs in which the college is considering offering CTE classes in order to project more accurately the numbers of students who would qualify if college or state policy requires qualifying GPAs or test scores. They could also ask high school principals to administer required tests early enough to provide prospective CTE students additional academic preparation and guidance if needed to qualify for CTE concurrent enrollment classes.

College administrators also must weigh the advantages and disadvantages of offering CTE concurrent enrollment classes that do not easily transfer in their state community college system. If CTE concurrent enrollment classes are offered, college administrators should be prepared not only to describe persuasively to students and instructors the benefits of taking free CTE concurrent enrollment classes that might not transfer but also to share information about increased earnings for college graduates. This is information that most of us take for granted but is probably not familiar to many CTE students who may not be planning to attend college.

Addressing Long-Term CTE Issues That Affect Students' Opportunities for Success. Another recommendation is that college administrators can organize colleagues and advocate for state support with the same tools used to educate the college community: educate policymakers about the long-term financial and academic benefits of concurrent enrollment. Finally, both secondary and postsecondary concurrent enrollment administrators could advocate for a mandate from states' Perkins plans that community colleges offer CTE concurrent enrollment classes, that all CTE students are required to take a minimum number of CTE concurrent enrollment classes, that classes are transferable within their state systems, and that classes are formally integrated with academic coursework for which both high school and college credit may be granted. With these foundational structures in place, CTE students who do not have clear plans to attend college could graduate from high school more prepared to excel in increasingly demanding workplaces or in college should they decide to attend.

References

Association for Career and Technical Education (ACTE). (2007, August). *CTE's role in secondary-postsecondary transitions* (ACTE Issue Brief). Retrieved from https://www.acteonline.org/uploadedFiles/Assets_and_Documents/Global/files/Publications/Transitions.pdf

Bishop-Clark, C., Hurn, J., Perry, S. A., Freeman, M. B., Jernigan, M., Wright, F., & Weldy, N. (2010). High school teachers teaching college courses to career technical education students? A story of success. *Journal of Career and Technical Education*, 25(2), 78–93.

Karp, M. M., Calcagno, J. C., Hughes, K. L., Jeong, D. W., & Bailey, T. R. (2007). *The postsecondary achievement of participants in dual enrollment: An analysis of student outcomes in two states*. New York, NY: Community College Research Center. Retrieved from   http://ccrc.tc.columbia.edu/media/k2/attachments/dual-enrollment-student-outcomes.pdf

National Research Center for Career and Technical Education (NRCCTE). (2010). *Professional development for secondary career and technical education: Implications for change*. Louisville, KY: University of Louisville. Retrieved from http://www.nrccte.org/sites/default/files/publication-files/professional_development_joint_2010.pdf

Stipanovic, N., Lewis, M. V., & Stringfield, S. (2012). Situating programs of study within current and historical career and technical educational reform efforts. *International Journal of Educational Reform*, 21, 80–97.

Zinth, J. D. (2013). Career/technical education: Not your father's vocational education. *The Progress of Education Reform*, 14(1), 1–7.

Zinth, J. D. (2014). *CTE dual enrollment: A strategy for college completion and workforce Investment*. Retrieved from http://www.ecs.org/clearinghouse/01/11/45/11150.pdf

PATRICIA W. HAAG *is a concurrent enrollment consultant who worked in that capacity at Southern Maine Community College from fall 2009 to spring 2014.*

NEW DIRECTIONS FOR COMMUNITY COLLEGES • DOI: 10.1002/cc

6

This chapter examines the experiences of five high school students previously enrolled in dual enrollment courses, and discusses the perceived benefits and disadvantages of these experiences from the student perspective.

Dual Enrollment Participation From the Student Perspective

M. Allison Kanny

As calls for enhanced K–16 pathways have gained currency in educational policy, dual enrollment has been found to provide support for a variety of students to not only enter, but excel in college (An, 2012; Karp & Hughes, 2008; Speroni, 2011; Struhl & Vargas, 2012). For these reasons, dual enrollment is receiving increased scrutiny by researchers and policymakers. The potential benefits of participating in dual enrollment courses span from immediate outcomes, such as improved high school grades, to comparatively longer term outcomes related to college academic performance and completion. Moreover, the benefits of dual enrollment course taking are becoming increasingly available to a wider range of students with respect to race/ethnicity, socioeconomic status, and prior academic achievement.

While the baseline outcomes of dual enrollment participation have been well established with respect to college performance and completion, relatively limited research has considered how or why these postsecondary outcomes tend to occur (Karp, 2007). The basis for increased rates of college completion for dual enrollment students takes different perspectives. One logic advanced in the research is that early college course-taking experiences are likely tied to increased familiarity and understanding of various aspects of college, academic and otherwise (Karp & Hughes, 2008). Karp's (2007) qualitative study of dually enrolled high school students revealed that early experiences in a college course led to earlier development of a "college student identity" that may have helped foster educational aspirations among students. Early exposure to college courses allows students to begin honing and developing necessary skills and coping strategies for college success such as advanced critical thinking and seeking instructor feedback (Hoffman, Vargas, & Santos, 2009). In turn, students are less likely

NEW DIRECTIONS FOR COMMUNITY COLLEGES, no. 169, Spring 2015 © 2015 Wiley Periodicals, Inc.
Published online in Wiley Online Library (wileyonlinelibrary.com) • DOI: 10.1002/cc.20133

to falter academically in the first semester and demonstrate greater persistence and completion rates compared to their similar ability peers (Struhl & Vargas, 2012).

While extant literature has begun to explore why and how dual enrollment affects students' outcomes by providing research related to discrete academic outcomes of dual enrollment participation (e.g., college grades), there is a need for more qualitative research on the student perspective regarding how dual enrollment participants perceive and experience the advantages and disadvantages of dual enrollment course taking. This chapter provides qualitative evidence by exploring how dually enrolled high school students within an urban setting conceptualize the benefits and drawbacks of dual enrollment participation using a qualitative, grounded theory approach. Using this student-centered approach, implications for policy and practice are then drawn in order to maximize the potential benefits of dual enrollment across an increasingly diverse student population.

Research Site and Participants

The site for this study was a small, independent charter school in an urban setting in Los Angeles, California. The school is situated in a low-income community, and 100% of the students qualify for the free and reduced lunch program. The high school consists of nearly 520 students and is 90% Latino. Beginning in the 2010–2011 academic year, high school sophomores and juniors in good academic standing began taking courses at a community college campus ("City College") located approximately 7 miles from the high school campus. Dually enrolled students were bused to the community college campus two to three days a week in order to attend courses. On average, these students were enrolled in two four-unit college courses per semester. Students were most often enrolled in mathematics and English language arts courses, though some reported taking courses related to politics and economics.

Five high school seniors who had taken dual enrollment courses as high school juniors self-selected to participate in this study. Four of the participants were female. All participants identified as Latina/o and had attended the charter school since the fifth grade. Moreover, each participant was considered "college-bound," having completed the A-G requirements as part of California's secondary curriculum. With respect to the participants' prior academic achievement, self-reports indicated that two students had earned unweighted grade point averages above 3.5, and the remaining three students reported earning grade point averages above 3.0.

Data Collection and Analysis

Each participant completed a demographic questionnaire that collected data regarding students' background characteristics, academic achievement in high school, and experiences in dual enrollment courses at City College. Participants also selected a pseudonym to be used for the study. Each student then participated in a one-on-one semistructured interview that lasted approximately 45–60 minutes. The semistructured nature of the interviews allowed for commonality across the interviews in terms of stem questions, while also providing flexibility to explore the unique aspects of each participant's perceptions of and experiences in dual enrollment courses (Miles & Huberman, 1994; Seidman, 1991).

As part of the data analysis process, all interviews were transcribed verbatim. Then in line with constant comparative analysis, transcripts were read multiple times with the goal of generating codes and patterns (Glaser & Strauss, 1967; Strauss & Corbin, 1994) that captured patterns in participants' experiences in courses at City College, general perceptions of the benefits of dual enrollment course taking, and reflections on disadvantages and areas for improvement in such course-taking experiences.

Findings

Findings revealed that students who participated in dual enrollment courses at City College perceived their experiences as simultaneously beneficial and detrimental to their academic achievement and personal growth as future college students. In particular, six themes emerged from the data, three each positively and negatively associated with students' participation in dual enrollment. Findings are grouped into the three themes that participants found beneficial and three themes that participants found detrimental, and are presented next.

Benefits of Dual Enrollment.   Three themes captured students' perceptions of benefits derived as a result of their dual enrollment experiences: exposure, learning the hidden curriculum, and independence and freedom.

Exposure.   A key theme that resonated among all participants focused on the benefits of being exposed to the college academic environment. Notably, despite separate accounts of particular courses taken at City College and their associated challenges, each participant referenced the undeniable importance of having the chance to experience the academic content and rigor of a college course.

As an example, when asked what the greatest benefit of taking courses as City College was, Roger responded without hesitation, "Exposure. Like just the fact that we were exposed to that kind of classroom setting." Explaining further, Roger relayed experiences as part of his college courses that were new to him:

> I liked it. It presented new things we'd never done before. For my history class, we had to turn in six-page papers . . . ten-page papers . . . fifteen-page papers. And I had never done that, so something new, you know? Like staying up all night trying to do an assignment. I had my first all-nighter!

Thus, taking part in college-level courses exposed Roger to course requirements (e.g., writing lengthy papers) that he had not previously encountered in his high school courses. Interestingly, Roger's reaction to this perceived increase in rigor was that of excitement and pride for having been faced with a new challenge and succeeding. Gloria, a straight-A student, also reflected on the impact of dual enrollment on affective outcomes such as academic self-confidence. She explained that despite her success in the high school academic environment, it was not until taking college courses that she was certain of her academic ability. She stated, "I think it boosts your morale, because you're taking classes with 23-year-olds." Similarly, other participants referenced a more general increase in their comfort levels pertaining to eventually applying to and attending college. "Just knowing now that I kind of know what it's like… it kind of made me feel better," said Gloria.

Roger also noted a change in his feelings toward college, but his were partially due to negative academic experiences. Specifically, Roger failed his computer science course. Additionally, in a course titled, "Administration of Justice," Roger excelled throughout the semester, earning a "high A" until the final exam. Due to his choice not to study for the exam, Roger failed the course final and ultimately earned a "D" in the course. Reflecting on this experience, he noted:

> And I think failing the classes was also … like … part of learning, you know? I think for me now… now I know. Like this isn't a joke, you know? This affects me. This is real. I had never failed a class until [City College]. I got my first C there too. I was really upset.

Importantly, despite the negative consequences of these courses as reflected by Roger's grades and his feelings about them, he still perceived these experiences as beneficial to his overall understanding of college academics. Roger adeptly summed his experiences up as ultimately positive, concluding, "I think I would have made these mistakes my first year, if I hadn't made them now."

Learning the Hidden Curriculum. An additional benefit of dual enrollment course participation as conceptualized by students was the chance to learn what is often referred to as "the hidden curriculum." The opportunity to take college courses resulted in the participants becoming aware of the more implicit skills and practices that are not only expected of college students, but also lead to enhanced academic success in college.

For example, participants noted learning about the importance of interacting with faculty on a regular basis. Alicia explained, "You really have to go talk to your professors. If you have a question, you just have to ask." After failing her computer science course, Alicia learned to "keep emailing the professor for help" the second time around. "I felt more comfortable. Because before, I was too scared and I just thought… nah, I just won't do [the homework]." In reference to how interactions with college professors differed from those with high school teachers, Carmen noted,

> With high school teachers ... they're just there. But at City College you have to go look for them. And if you don't go, they just assume you don't need help. They're not going to look for you. And [at the charter school], they babysit us too much.

Moreover, Cecilia explained, "If [high school teachers] see that the class is struggling, they'll make a review, and they'll make you study. But in college, they don't care. It's like, if you're failing, it's your problem. It's on you." Accordingly, it seems that high school students benefited from dual enrollment course taking by becoming acclimated to differences in student–instructor interactions at the college level that foster academic success.

Other hidden curriculum competencies that students derived from taking courses at City College included learning about their own learning styles. Cecilia reflected on how taking college courses forced her to explore different ways to learn and to ultimately determine which ways worked best for her. She explained that upon approaching a professor for help, she was told that it was important for her to work with the course material "outside of class in [her] own way." As a result, Cecilia began to look up her math course content on Google rather than using the course textbook. She recalled, "I didn't know how to do that. In high school, we always just do things one way ... however the teacher teaches us. I learned about the best ways I learn. It gave me a new studying habit."

Similarly, referring to her computer science course, Alicia relayed initial issues in understanding the course syllabus and requirements. She stated,

> The professor would just put a Powerpoint up and leave and say, 'Just do your assignments.' So I was like ... ok cool. And next thing I knew I found out we were supposed to have turned in all our assignments online, and I never figured that out, so I failed.

In order to replace this failing grade on her transcript, Alicia had to retake the computer science course independently of the high school arrangements with City College. Alicia revealed that she retook the course as part of a night course series, had very positive interactions with the professor, and passed the course with an "A."

Independence and Freedom. A final theme related to students' perceived benefits of dual enrollment course taking entailed learning to be more independent within the context of academics. Each participant specifically noted the words "independence" and "freedom" during the interviews. Interestingly, participants tended to discuss this notion of gaining independence as a dissonant experience in which overcoming fear was often a major component. According to Alicia, "I think [taking college courses in high school] gives you independence. I was completely on my own, and I had no one to help me. I was really scared. I now know what it feels like if I was actually in college." Cecilia also underscored the independence associated with dual enrollment, mentioning,

> No one was there. And it was like we were really kind of experiencing that . . . that college life. Like having to interact with people who you knew nothing about. It matured me because it broadened my view on what [taking college courses] is actually going to be like.

Participants also discussed independence in terms of gaining "freedom" from the more structured high school academic setting. Often, these students noted reacting poorly to this newfound leniency. Gloria noted, "They basically chose us [to take DE courses] because they assumed we were the most responsible students, and the most mature. But once it came to having that freedom, it was like . . . woohoo!" Cecilia elaborated on such freedom in her interview:

> I think I didn't take it seriously. I was like . . . 'Oh, I'm in 11th grade and I'm taking college courses.' And I had so much more freedom. Like literally I would go out during class, buy a burger, and bring it back to class and eat it. I feel so disrespectful now, now that I think about it.

Others spoke of the element of freedom and its negative impact on their grades. Referring to why he failed his computer science course, Roger said,

> I think it's just the freedom. You get so much freedom, and I didn't know what to do with it. You feel grown up. And you give freedom to a sixteen-year-old and they're like 'I don't care, I'm just going to go do what I want.'

Thus, exposure to increased independence and freedom in college-level courses presented challenges to participants; however, they spoke of these challenges in positive ways. In other words, participants viewed the opportunity to encounter such new experiences as ultimately helpful and important to their future success as college students.

Drawbacks of Dual Enrollment.   Three themes captured students' perceptions of drawbacks as a result of their dual enrollment experiences: issues in credit and grades, negative interactions with others, and limited support systems.

Issues in Credit and Grades.   The most prevalent theme related to the drawbacks of dual enrollment was issues in credits earned as well as negative impacts on high school transcripts due to poor grades in dual enrollment courses. The students explained that earning dual credit was important to them and a key reason for taking courses at City College. "The fact that we were taking college courses, period, that was like . . . those are going to be on our high school transcripts, that's obviously going to look good," said Cecilia. Gloria also elaborated this point by describing what the high school administrators told students about taking dual enrollment courses. "They told us, 'You're going to get college credit … You'll be able to enter as a sophomore instead of a freshman … You'll save so much money … You'll get into better colleges,'" recalled Gloria.

Unfortunately, participants consistently referenced incongruences in the college courses they took and the credits they needed on their high school transcripts. Further, there was notable frustration in their discussion of taking courses that did not contribute to their high school transcripts. Gloria noted, "They made us take all these classes that didn't even count. Like yeah, sure, half of my classes don't even help me now … they don't. Like the PE class and the history class that didn't even count." Similarly, Cecilia lamented,

> It turns out that we are going to start out like everyone else as freshman. They didn't even give us college credit. We just completed the A through G requirements we needed for high school. Just because we didn't have those classes here.

These statements reflect a general sense of frustration with unmet assurances that taking courses at City College would assist students in earning college credits prior to high school graduation.

Students also consistently cited earning failing grades or grades that were significantly lower than those they typically earned in high school courses. Notably, three student participants reported failing one or more courses at City College. The other two participants reported that the lowest grades they received were a "C" and a "D." Carmen discussed the negative impact of earning failing and below average grades in terms of her high school transcript. Specifically, she estimated that her high school GPA might have been close to an unweighted 4.0 had she taken all courses within the high school. She went on to postulate how college admissions counselors will eventually perceive her transcript with uncertainty. She ultimately concluded, however, "I don't think [dual enrollment] benefited me at all, because I think you see those grades and they just look really bad." Alicia's perception of the negative impacts of earning low grades at City College also involved anxiety over how these grades would be interpreted. "It just bumped my GPA so low … it just really makes me worried," said Alicia.

Negative Interactions With Others.   Students also experienced negative impacts from their dual enrollment experiences due to negative interactions with others on the City College campus. A majority of participants mentioned feeling uncomfortable due to their nontraditional enrollment status. Specifically, they referenced feelings of being judged by students and faculty at City College. Cecilia recalled, "We were looked down upon in a way. It was kind of friendly joking, but people were like, 'Oh, you think you're all smart just because you take classes at City College?'" The students noted feelings of a chilly classroom environment with respect to other students. "They didn't like us. They would give us faces," said Roger. Cecilia reflected that, "They might have felt threatened. Or it seemed like they were upset that we were taking up space."

Participants explained differing reactions to these negative experiences with other students. Alicia recalled, "I was in my [school] uniform and everyone else was like, 'What are you doing here?'" She eventually dropped the class, based on her reaction to these negative interactions. She said, "I just didn't want to do it. I just wanted to be in high school." Roger persisted in the courses he took at City College, but took a more reflective stance when speaking of his experiences. "Now that I think about it, the other student might have been right. We weren't very mature. There were times we would be in the library messing around. We thought we were grown up because they gave us the opportunity to be there, but we weren't," said Roger.

Pertaining to City College faculty, participants referenced numerous instances in which faculty made explicit remarks about their dislike of teaching high school students. Gloria stated, "The professors didn't like us. They thought we were immature. They even said things like, 'I came to teach college students. If I wanted to teach high school students, I'd be teaching at a high school.'" Cecelia explained feelings of discomfort due to faculty's remarks such as that mentioned above. She revealed,

> It was scary because I didn't know if I was going to be alone for the duration of the class. Like what if I need help? I was too shy and scared after I heard [a professor] make a negative remark about high school students taking college courses.

Thus, students tended to report negative interactions with others at City College that had detrimental effects on their feelings of comfort on campus and course performance.

Limited Support Systems.   There was limited support from the high school or community college in ensuring students stayed on track. For instance, once students were enrolled in courses at City College, there was little interaction between high school personnel and the students related to dual enrollment courses. Roger noted, "[High school counselors] would check up on you, but as long as you're in your class, you're fine. You're on your own. If you turned in that assignment or not, it doesn't matter ... no one's on your tail about it." As previously mentioned, Roger noted doing very well in his administration of justice course until the final, which he did not study for. Unfortunately, despite the fact that Roger had an A going into the final, he failed the final exam and received a D in the course. In reference to this experience, he mentioned, "I don't know. I didn't do it [study for the final] because I didn't feel like it, and no one really was telling me to." Other participants relayed similar experiences in their own dual enrollment courses, often returning to the theme of limited support from the high school in helping them to navigate new challenges and norms of college-level courses.

In other instances, students mentioned feeling isolated from the City College community. These feelings of isolation led to uncertainty regarding their feelings of belonging at the institution. Gloria emphasized issues related to college faculty. "They expected us to know all this stuff that we just didn't know," said Gloria while referring to her experience being placed into a trigonometry course without having taken geometry. "I passed, but barely and it just made me feel like I shouldn't be there because there were all these things I hadn't done there yet," said Gloria. Additionally, Alicia explained,

> I guess I didn't feel like an actual student. Like I didn't want to go to the library because I wasn't a student. I didn't go to tutoring because I wasn't a student. Other students could go and talk to the counselor or go and have a tutoring session.

In fact, a number of participants highlighted feeling that they were not able to access some support services. For example, Carmen mentioned that she could not attend the tutoring sessions because they were scheduled at times when the high school students were not on campus at City College. Based on these recollections, paired with the limited support received from the high school, it was clear that these participants felt generally unsupported and isolated in their tenure at City College, and asserted that these feelings were detrimental to the quality of their experiences there.

Conclusion and Implications

This exploratory qualitative study examined the perceptions of students regarding the benefits and drawbacks of dual enrollment. While limited in scope to five participants attending a small charter school in Los Angeles, California, this study makes an important contribution to what is currently known about the impact of dual enrollment because it focuses on the student perspective. Dual enrollment is increasingly perceived and promoted as a strategy for increasing the college-readiness and success of a wide range of high school students, including those who are traditionally underrepresented in higher education.

What is readily evident from the findings of this study is that students potentially experience a wide range of benefits and drawbacks simultaneously while taking dual enrollment courses. The intersection between positive and negative experiences was also very apparent. That is, students' reflections on the benefits and drawbacks of dual enrollment were

New Directions for Community Colleges • DOI: 10.1002/cc

not mutually exclusive. For example, students were particularly pleased by the level of exposure to college-level academics they received by taking classes at City College, but were simultaneously disappointed by the negative interactions with others they faced within those same classes. Similarly, students spoke of the positive impacts of learning about the degree of independence and freedom that college courses entail, but cited a number of examples in which these positive aspects of dual enrollment led to severe setbacks in their high school transcripts. Although not unexpected, the high level of nuance and intersection among students' perceived benefits and drawbacks of dual enrollment warrants mention.

Given that students' experiences in dual enrollment courses are inclusive of this mixture of positive and negative experiences, a logical next question arises: how can high school and community college faculty and administrators enhance the benefits of dual enrollment while minimizing the drawbacks? At the secondary level, two implications are drawn from this study. First, it is clear that more work needs to be done to help manage students' expectations regarding college academics *prior* to their matriculation into dual enrollment courses. The participants in this study all noted feelings of pride at having been exposed to college courses prior to graduating from high school. However, they also revealed that a number of experiences at City College were unexpected in terms of their preparation for dual enrollment. For example, students were unfamiliar with college norms surrounding coursework, grading practices, and interaction with professors. As a result, the learning curve was especially steep for these participants with respect to becoming acclimated to basic college academic norms. Moreover, most participants experienced negative outcomes in their grades and credits earned as a result. With improved preparation at the high school level, students would be better equipped to manage new academic experiences at the college level. Simply put, the learning curve need not be so steep for dual enrollment students if only their home schools dedicated energy to preparing students for these experiences.

Concurrently, more work is needed at the college level to help shape and manage college professors' expectations of dual enrollment students. The participants in this study consistently cited having interactions with faculty members who were skeptical of, if not averse to, teaching high school students. Given that dual enrollment students seem to be at risk for experiencing a relatively unwelcoming environment, more positive interactions with college professors would likely help to assuage students' feelings of discomfort. More targeted dual enrollment professional development opportunities for faculty and staff at postsecondary institutions could be implemented to help build greater buy-in among individuals who will encounter dual enrollment students. Further, such professional development opportunities would help professors to become more attuned to some of the instructional scaffolding or adaptations that would help dual enrollment students (e.g., more explicit explanation of syllabi).

NEW DIRECTIONS FOR COMMUNITY COLLEGES • DOI: 10.1002/cc

Finally, students' discussion of the limited support received from their high school staff during their time at City College underscores the need for more purposeful and structured support systems to be implemented for dual enrollment students. With respect to community colleges, the provision of student services might be adapted to better suit the needs of a wider range of students with varying schedules. For example, tutoring services could be offered at times or in alternative modes such that dual enrollment students can access them. Additionally, some supervision of students via the work of counselors, teachers, or professors should be ongoing during students' tenure at the college. However, it is important to note that practitioners must endeavor to provide this support while preserving the level of "freedom" and "independence" that dual enrollment students explained as a benefit of their experiences.

Given the community college's ever-expanding mission and role as a provider of educational opportunity to a variety of students, it is prudent that scholars and practitioners begin to better understand the ways that dual enrollment functions as an agent of college access and success. If we know more about this dynamic, researchers, practitioners, and policymakers alike can begin to better wield the dual enrollment tool to achieve enhanced college academic outcomes and persistence among various students. This, in turn, will enable greater efficiency and efficacy at the community college to better serve its student population and more adequately fulfill its many missions.

References

An, B. (2012). The impact of dual enrollment on college degree attainment: Do low-SES student benefit? *Educational Evaluation and Policy Analysis, 35*(1), 57–75.

Glaser, B. G., & Strauss, A. L. (1967). *The discovery of grounded theory: Strategies for qualitative research*. Chicago, IL: Aldine.

Hoffman, N., Vargas, J., & Santos, J. (2009). New directions for dual enrollment: Creating stronger pathways from high school through college. In A. C. Bueschel & A. Venezia (Eds.), *New Directions for Community Colleges: No. 145. Policies and practice to improve student preparation and success* (pp. 43–58). San Francisco, CA: Jossey-Bass.

Karp, M. M. (2007). *Learning about the role of college student through dual enrollment participation* (CCRC Working Paper No. 7). New York, NY: Community College Research Center, Teachers College, Columbia University.

Karp, M. M., & Hughes, K. L. (2008). Dual enrollment can benefit a broad range of students. *Techniques: Connecting Education and Careers, 83*(7), 14–17.

Miles, M. B., & Huberman, A. M. (1994). *Qualitative data analysis: A sourcebook of new methods*. Beverly Hills, CA: Sage.

Seidman, I. E. (1991). *Interviewing as qualitative research: A guide for researchers in education & the social sciences*. New York, NY: Teachers College Press.

Speroni, C. (2011, November). *Determinants of students' success: The role of advanced placement and dual enrollment programs*. National Center for Postsecondary Research. Community College Research Center: Columbia University. Retrieved from http://www.postsecondaryresearch.org/index.html?Id=Publications&Info=NCPR+Publications

Strauss, A., & Corbin, J. (1994). Grounded theory methodology: An overview. In N. K. Denzin & Y. S. Lincoln (Eds.), *Handbook of qualitative research* (pp. 273–285). Thousand Oaks, CA: Sage.

Struhl, B., & Vargas, J. (2012). *Taking college courses in high school: A strategy for college readiness*. Boston, MA: Jobs for the Future.

M. ALLISON KANNY *is a research analyst at Cypress College.*

7

The purpose of this chapter is to describe teacher, counselor, and principal perceptions of a concurrent enrollment program collaboratively administered by a large, Midwestern community college and area high schools. Data come from surveys sent to these stakeholders as part of concurrent enrollment program accreditation through National Association of Concurrent Enrollment Partnerships.

Principal, Teacher, and Counselor Views of Concurrent Enrollment

Jana M. Hanson, Todd Prusha, Cort Iverson

What do school professionals think about concurrent enrollment? We conducted a study of 150 high school principals, guidance counselors, and concurrent enrollment instructors from 35 high schools. The responses from the surveys help us understand concurrent enrollment from the perspective of these educational professionals. The survey responses reveal how teachers, counselors, and principals view the impact of concurrent enrollment classes on their school environment and students. Although teachers, counselors, and principals are deeply involved in the day-to-day operations and delivery of concurrent enrollment programming, we know little about their thoughts on its impact.

Much of the literature on concurrent enrollment programs focuses on the students participating in postsecondary coursework while still in high school. For example, Karp (2012) developed a theoretical framework focused on college readiness in order to more fully understand the student experience of concurrent enrollment courses. Researchers have also evaluated students' perceptions of concurrent enrollment programs. In general, students find these programs useful, motivating, and satisfying (Allen & Dadgar, 2012; Orr, 2002; Peterson, Anjewierden, & Corser, 2001; Robertson, Chapman, & Gaskin, 2001). Peterson et al. (2001) found that less than 3% of students in their sample were unsatisfied with concurrent enrollment coursework. In addition, Lewis (2009) focused on the perceptions of students regarding concurrent enrollment program participation in high school and their subsequent university experience. Although the

NEW DIRECTIONS FOR COMMUNITY COLLEGES, no. 169, Spring 2015 © 2015 Wiley Periodicals, Inc.
Published online in Wiley Online Library (wileyonlinelibrary.com) • DOI: 10.1002/cc.20134

majority of students had already planned to attend college after high school prior to enrolling in the concurrent enrollment program, students reported many positive experiences. Some of the positive experiences students reported included utilizing additional campus resources, such as the college's tutoring and library services. Students also suggested that by participating in a concurrent enrollment course, they were more confident, comfortable, and prepared for a college setting (Lewis, 2009).

While students are the center of concurrent enrollment programs, other constituents are actively involved in shaping the success of programs. Instructors at either the high school or local community college follow the specified curriculum and manage their courses. In addition, high school counselors coordinate schedules and ensure student awareness, registration, and participation in the program. Finally, high school principals are responsible for decisions about school involvement with a concurrent enrollment program.

Although teachers, counselors, and principals are vital to the success of a concurrent enrollment program, there is little information published that evaluates how these three groups perceive such a program. This chapter focused on how teachers, counselors, and principals perceive the benefits—to both their schools and students—of a concurrent enrollment program. The results from the study have important implications from an institutional perspective, including grant and professional development opportunities, as well as program improvement.

Concurrent Enrollment Program at Kirkwood Community College

Kirkwood Community College (Kirkwood) is a large, Midwestern community college in Iowa. Concurrent enrollment classes in Iowa are regulated by legislation entitled "Senior Year Plus" (State of Iowa, Department of Education, 2008). Local school districts cover tuition costs of their students in college credit classes. High schools that partner with National Association of Concurrent Enrollment Partnerships (NACEP) accredited community colleges to offer concurrent enrollment classes are awarded supplemental funding from the state. Kirkwood's program is NACEP accredited and accounts for approximately 10% of concurrent enrollment students in Iowa. In 2012–2013, Kirkwood enrolled 3,631 concurrent enrollment students and offered 769 course sections. All 42 high schools in Kirkwood's region enrolled students in concurrent enrollment courses.

Kirkwood has long acknowledged the essential role teachers, counselors, and principals play in the success of the concurrent enrollment program. Concurrent enrollment teachers from area high schools participate in professional development opportunities such as training in using the learning management system, integrating technology into the classroom, and engaging students in the specific academic discipline activities and projects. The teachers use such training to enhance their concurrent enrollment courses. Additionally, teachers exchange teaching strategies, as well as sharing resources and forming a feeling of consistency and belonging from networking with other concurrent teachers and community college faculty. Kirkwood also understands the vital role counselors play. Counselors are responsible for the collaboration and communication between Kirkwood and the high school site. Counselors are not only the central point of contact for students enrolling in concurrent class, but they are also the central point of contact with community college staff. Without the support and legwork of the high school guidance counselors, concurrent enrollment courses would not exist. In addition, high school principals pave the way to make the concurrent enrollment programs successful by promoting, valuing, and offering the programs in their schools. Because the high school teachers, counselors, and principals are essential to the success of concurrent enrollment programs, their perceptions are important to better understand the impact these programs have on schools and students. Our community college program directors and coordinators solicit and use these perceptions and feedback to enhance program offerings and increase student success.

As a measure of good practice and keeping in line with NACEP standards, Kirkwood surveys concurrent enrollment students, teachers, guidance counselors, and principals. Data from these surveys are used to improve programming, partnership procedures, and student success. In this chapter, we explore how teachers, counselors, and principals perceive benefits for their schools and students from participation in our concurrent enrollment program. Information from the teacher, counselor, and principal survey is used to address the two important questions:

1. How do teachers, counselors, and principals perceive concurrent enrollment programs impact their schools?
2. How do teachers, counselors, and principals perceive concurrent enrollment programs impact their students?

Survey Methods

Every three years, Kirkwood sends surveys to concurrent enrollment program teachers, counselors, and principals to assist us in understanding their experiences and perceptions. We used items from NACEP (http://www.nacep.org/accreditation/forms-resources/) to design these surveys. Some items used for our surveys focused on the impact of concurrent enrollment on the high school such as offering rigorous classes, enhancing school prestige, and raising expectations for student performance. Other survey items related to how concurrent enrollment courses impacted students, including whether respondents thought concurrent enrollment courses improved students' study skills, and increased college expectations and educational aspirations. For most items, respondents indicated the extent they agreed or disagreed with a statement (5 = strongly agree, 4 = agree, 3 = neutral, 2 = disagree, and 1 = strongly disagree). The percentages derived in Tables 7.1 and 7.2 collapse (5) strongly agree and (4) agree into the heading "% Agree." The same category collapsing is presented in Tables 7.1 and 7.2 for (1) strongly disagree and (2) disagree to "% Disagree." In addition to the percentage agree and disagree ratings, open-ended items allowed respondents to describe the impact concurrent enrollment courses have on their high schools and students.

For this chapter, we used the most recent survey data based on electronic surveys sent to teachers, counselors, and principals in late May 2013. The sampling frame was composed of 244 teachers, 78 counselors, and 41 principals at the 42 high schools who participated in Kirkwood's concurrent enrollment program. Of these, 117 teachers (48.0% response rate), 27 counselors (34.6% response rate), and 20 principals (48.8% response rate) completed the survey.

Impact on Schools

Our first research question sought to understand how teachers, counselors, and principals perceive the concurrent enrollment programs impact their schools. It should be noted that while the questions asked respondents to specifically consider how concurrent enrollment impacts their schools, respondents tended to focus on students. Respondents may not have identified a distinction between schools and students. Perhaps benefits to the students are also benefits to the schools and vice versa.

In general, the respondents strongly agreed or agreed that the concurrent enrollment program had a positive impact on their schools (results reported in Table 7.1). The survey item with the largest percentage of respondents agreeing was the school offers prerequisite courses that prepare students for college courses (85%). The survey item with the lowest percentage of respondents agreeing was the school has more students continuing on to postsecondary education (63%).

Our respondents provided qualitative comments on the positive impact concurrent enrollment courses have on their schools. In particular, several respondents commented that these programs provide high schools with the ability to allow students to earn college credits while in high school and better prepare students for college-level work. For example, one teacher wrote, "It gives our students exposure to learning opportunities before they get to college." Another teacher commented that "many more students [are] being prepared for college with credits earned, classes offered, and experienced gained." A principal said, "Students have the opportunity to experience college-level courses and to earn college-level credit while in high school." A counselor stated the program allows "our student to graduate with some required college classes under their belt. It also give[s] them a better idea of what they'll...be dealing with in college." In general, the

Table 7.1 Perspectives on the Benefits of Concurrent Enrollment Programs on Schools

	All Groups			Teachers			Counselors			Principals		
	% Agree	% Neutral	% Disagree	% Agree	% Neutral	% Disagree	% Agree	% Neutral	% Disagree	% Agree	% Neutral	% Disagree
Implementing college course standards	82	15	3	83	14	4	74	22	4	90	10	—
Expecting college level work	83	12	4	87	9	4	67	26	7	85	10	5
Has more students continuing on to postsecondary education	63	34	3	61	35	4	59	37	4	75	25	—
Raises expectations for student performance in courses preceding concurrent enrollment program courses	70	23	7	69	24	7	62	27	12	85	15	—
Demonstrates to parents that their students are doing challenging work	79	19	2	82	15	3	67	33	—	80	20	—
Offers prerequisite courses that prepare students for college courses	85	12	3	86	10	4	70	30	—	100	—	—
Enhances its prestige and academic reputation	81	17	2	83	15	2	67	30	4	90	10	—
Offers more rigorous classes	76	20	4	79	18	3	59	30	11	80	20	—
Requiring higher level of student accountability	80	17	3	82	15	4	74	26	—	75	20	5
Has more students succeed in postsecondary education	65	33	2	64	35	1	67	26	7	70	30	—

Participant Type

Table 7.2 Perspectives on the Benefits of Concurrent Enrollment Programs on Students

	Participant Type											
	All Groups			Teachers			Counselors			Principals		
	% Agree	% Neutral	% Disagree	% Agree	% Neutral	% Disagree	% Agree	% Neutral	% Disagree	% Agree	% Neutral	% Disagree
Developed a good understanding of their academic skills	74	21	4	76	20	4	62	31	8	83	17	–
Develop realistic expectations of college	77	17	7	77	16	7	69	23	8	83	11	6
Raise their educational aspirations	65	33	2	65	33	2	58	38	4	78	22	–
Have enrolled in academically challenging courses	66	28	6	67	27	6	48	44	8	89	11	–
Considered, for the first time, going to college	35	51	14	31	56	13	38	38	23	56	39	6
Are staying on the high school campus instead of attending college courses at another site	61	28	10	61	27	12	60	32	8	65	29	6
Increase their likelihood of pursuing postsecondary education	67	29	4	65	31	4	62	31	8	83	17	–
Gained in-depth knowledge in the subject area	92	6	2	92	5	3	85	15	–	100	–	–
Participate in rigorous learning	86	9	4	90	6	4	69	23	8	88	12	–
Developed effective study skills	62	33	5	60	33	7	62	35	4	72	28	–
Developed effective time management skills	68	28	5	67	27	7	65	35	–	78	22	–

open-ended responses tended to focus on earning college credits and gaining a college-like experience.

Our survey did not focus on the financial benefits of concurrent enrollment programs. However, several respondents identified the pecuniary advantage of the concurrent enrollment program for students. For example, one principal stated a benefit of concurrent enrollment was "saving family money on college tuition expenses." A counselor said, "Students earn college credit they don't have to pay for later." From these responses, respondents identified that concurrent enrollment provides students with an opportunity to save money by taking college credits in high school.

In addition to the question about impact on school, we were also interested in evaluating whether the three respondent groups (teachers, counselors, and principals) differed in their perceived impact of the concurrent enrollment program on their school. There were statistically significant differences on the following three school impact survey items: (a) Kirkwood's concurrent enrollment courses improved academic rigor in my school by expecting college-level work; (b) as a result of offering concurrent enrollment courses, my school enhances its prestige and academic reputation; and (c) as a result of offering concurrent enrollment courses, my school offers more rigorous classes. For all three items, counselors tended to agree less compared to teachers and principals. This may be due to the different functions for which each group is responsible. Unlike the teachers and principals, counselors tend to focus on administrative tasks, such as registration, grade reporting, and concern about student soft skills and overall social–emotional impact. Counselors may have less awareness related to the specific academic content and level of work in the concurrent classroom.

Impact on Students

The second question addressed in this chapter sought to understand how teachers, counselors, and principals perceive concurrent enrollment programs impact their students. Overall, respondents strongly agreed or agreed that the concurrent enrollment program had a positive impact on their students. The survey item with the greatest percentage of respondents agreeing was that students gained in-depth knowledge in subject areas (92%). The survey item with the lowest percentage of respondents agreeing was that the student considered for the first time going to college (35%). This may be because most students already had plans to attend college prior to participating in the concurrent enrollment program.

Teachers, counselors, and principals provided additional comments on the perceived impacts of the concurrent enrollment programs on students. Respondents' comments focused mostly on how concurrent enrollment allows students to earn college credit and take college-level courses. For example, one principal stated that the greatest impact of concurrent enrollment was "providing [students with] an opportunity to experience college-level classes and to earn college credit." One teacher said that the students "are more prepared for college and beyond, and have a head start as they are earning college credits while in high school." In general, teachers, counselors, and principals considered the opportunities of gaining college credit and experiencing college-level courses to be an important outcome for students and an important part of their transition to college.

Respondents, teachers especially, focused on another theme related to increased rigor and expectations of courses. For example, one teacher said, "the exposure to math topics they never would have seen in their high school math studies has impacted my student[s] as well as upping their interest level" in math. Another teacher stated, "[Students] discover how much harder they must work for a college course than what they are used to doing when they were younger . . . but that they can do it." From these observations, stakeholders believe that concurrent enrollment programs provide students with more challenging coursework and expectations that they otherwise would not have been exposed to prior to high school graduation.

Survey comments from counselors and teachers pointed to both the personal and academic gains of concurrent enrollment. For example, one counselor said that concurrent enrollment had the greatest impact on students' "learning time management and academic problem solving skills." Another counselor said the program helps build "academic and personal confidence." Likewise, one counselor mentioned students "gaining confidence in their abilities." One teacher stated, "Students develop time management and study skills to better prepare them for college . . ." These statements suggest that concurrent enrollment programs may prepare students to be college-ready by providing both personal and academic skills.

We were also interested in evaluating whether the three respondent groups (teachers, counselors, and principals) differed on the perceived impact of concurrent enrollment on students. There were significant differences on the following two survey items: (a) as a result of the presence of concurrent enrollment courses in my school, more students have enrolled in academically challenging courses; and (b) as a result of taking concurrent enrollment courses in my high school, students participate in rigorous learning. Counselors again tended to agree less with these items compared to teachers and principals. As previously indicated, counselors may be more concerned with personal and academic skills and less concerned about the academic rigor of the courses than teachers and principals.

Discussions, Implications, and Conclusions

This chapter provided insights into the perceptions of teachers, counselors, and principals regarding concurrent enrollment programs. The three groups generally perceived concurrent enrollment to have positive benefits for both the schools and students. In particular, schools and students benefited from increased student preparation for future college-level coursework and gaining in-depth knowledge in subject areas. Students are able to earn college credit and take college-level courses. Students also make personal and academic gains by participating in a concurrent enrollment course. There were some differences between the groups. Teachers were significantly more likely than counselors to perceive concurrent enrollment increased rigorous class offerings and expectations for college-level work at high schools, as well as student participation in rigorous learning. Principals were also significantly more likely than counselors to perceive concurrent enrollment increased student participation in academically challenging courses. In both cases, the counselors expressed less agreement with the academic benefits than teachers and principals.

The differences that were found likely highlight the distinct role each stakeholder plays relative to concurrent enrollment. The teachers serve as frontline educators and may be more attuned to course content and how it compares to high school level work, but may be less concerned with students' specific enrollment choices than principals and counselors. Counselors serve as liaisons between the community college, the high school, and students, and therefore they have a broader perspective of the concurrent enrollment program and focus more on coordination than the academic dimensions of concurrent enrollment. Finally, principals—focused on educational administration—are indirectly involved with the day-to-day details of concurrent enrollment. As such, they may be more focused on patterns of enrollment and consider concurrent enrollment courses to be more academically rigorous than standard high school courses.

The perspectives and feedback from teachers, counselors, and principals are useful on several dimensions. First, teachers, counselors, and principals are crucial in ensuring the success of concurrent enrollment programs. As such, their perceptions of how these programs impact their schools and students are important and useful. For example, respondent's comments did not focus on concurrent enrollment courses' influence on students' decisions to continue on to postsecondary education. Instead, it may be that students who were already planning to go to college participate in concurrent enrollment courses. Because one of the goals of concurrent enrollment programs is to encourage all high school students to continue to postsecondary education, Kirkwood used these data as the basis for a grant opportunity to provide funding for a summer bridge program for non-college-bound students. This bridge program is an important partnership between the community college and local high schools. The summer bridge program is designed to help prepare 9th and 10th graders to take concurrent enrollment classes as 11th and 12th graders. Research shows that students who participated in a concurrent enrollment program have higher college GPAs, are less likely to take a remedial math course, and are more likely to persist and attain a degree, so it is our hope that the summer bridge program will increase the number of postsecondary education–bound high school students in our region.

NEW DIRECTIONS FOR COMMUNITY COLLEGES • DOI: 10.1002/cc

The information from the Kirkwood survey also provides insights into how to assist teachers, counselors, and principals. Our concurrent enrollment program relies heavily on coordination efforts by these three groups. Kirkwood uses the data from this survey to plan and prepare professional development opportunities for individuals involved with the concurrent enrollment program. These activities focus on content-rich curricula and general educational learning activities. Feedback is collected following these professional development activities, and comments from follow-up surveys indicate two main areas for program enhancement. Respondents most appreciate the opportunity to participate in discipline-specific peer discussion and collegial sharing with other concurrent enrollment instructors and community college faculty. Additionally, more time is requested to focus on technology training and technology solutions for the classroom- and discipline-specific teaching and learning.

In addition to teacher professional development, Kirkwood also hosts monthly partnership meetings with the high school counselors and principals for program administration and planning of future course offerings and professional development. Feedback from our partnership meetings is focused toward two main areas. First, principals and counselors prefer to meet in a face-to-face environment. Web meetings are not well attended and respondents report an inability to concentrate due to school/office environment interruptions. Second, in addition to routine business matters, principals and counselors prefer for our partnership meetings to include an opportunity for tours, information sessions, and college guest speakers.

Finally, in regard to our teacher, counselor, and principal survey, it was invaluable to include the Department of Institutional Research in the process. Institutional Research was able to assist in fine-tuning the survey, improving survey response rates, and compiling data into useful reports. In addition, Institutional Research provided guidance in interpreting and using the results. The collaboration between Institutional Research and the concurrent enrollment program coordinator led to rich dialogue and brainstorming related to program improvement.

Further surveys are warranted to continue exploring the perceptions of teachers, counselors, and principals involved in concurrent enrollment programs. In particular, it is of value to more fully understand how each of these groups may benefit professionally from participating in concurrent enrollment programs. For instance, how does participation in concurrent enrollment instruction and professional development impact the nonconcurrent classes taught by these same high school teachers? Does the information gained through the college-offered concurrent professional development carry over into the nonconcurrent high school courses? Is this professional development information shared with nonconcurrent instructors in the high school? Would the entire high school instructional staff, concurrent and nonconcurrent enrollment, be interested in participating in the professional development and collegial sharing offered by the community college–sponsored activities? How do the high school professionals feel the community college professional development compares to their high school specific professional development? Do the high school professionals feel the community college faculty could benefit from the high school professional development training topics? Creating a seamless, secondary/postsecondary educational community is a benefit of our concurrent enrollment programs at Kirkwood Community College. Knowing how our concurrent enrollment activities and partnering practices impact high school concurrent enrollment professionals and students is of great value in strengthening our community.

References

Allen, D., & Dadgar, M. (2012). Does dual enrollment increase students' success in college? Evidence from a quasi-experimental analysis of dual enrollment in New York City. In E. Hoffman & D. Voloch (Eds.), *New Directions for Higher Education: No. 158. Dual enrollment: Strategies, outcomes, and lessons for school–college partnerships* (pp. 11–19). San Francisco, CA: Jossey-Bass.

Karp, M. M. (2012). "I don't know, I've never been to college!" Dual enrollment as a college readiness strategy. In E. Hoffman & D. Voloch (Eds.), *New Directions for Higher Education: No. 158. Dual enrollment: Strategies, outcomes, and lessons for school–college partnerships* (pp. 21–28). San Francisco, CA: Jossey-Bass.

Lewis, T. L. (2009). *Student reflections: The impact of dual enrollment on transitions to a state university* (Doctoral dissertation). University of South Florida, Tampa, FL.

Orr, M. T. (2002, April). *Dual enrollment: Developments, trends and impacts.* Presentation to the Community College Research Center, Teachers College, Columbia University.

Peterson, M., Anjewierden, J., & Corser, C. (2001). Designing an effective concurrent enrollment program: A focus on quality of instruction and student outcomes. In P. F. Robertson, B. G. Chapman, & F. Gaskin (Eds.), *New Directions for Community Colleges: No. 113. Systems for offering concurrent enrollment at high schools and community colleges* (pp. 23–32). San Francisco, CA: Jossey-Bass.

Robertson, P. F., Chapman, B. G., & Gaskin, F. (Eds.). (2001). *New Directions for Community Colleges: No. 113. Systems for offering concurrent enrollment at high schools and community colleges.* San Francisco, CA: Jossey-Bass.

State of Iowa, Department of Education. (2008). *Senior Year Plus Program* (Iowa Code Chapter 261E). Retrieved from https://www.educateiowa.gov/sites/files/ed/documents/2008-09-25%20Guidance%20on%20House%20File%202679%20-%20Senior%20Year%20Plus.pdf

JANA M. HANSON is a research analyst at Kirkwood Community College.

TODD PRUSHA is the dean for distance learning at Kirkwood Community College.

CORT IVERSON is the director for institutional research at Kirkwood Community College.

This chapter presents the results of a study that investigated faculty members' views on the level of academic rigor in three settings at one community college: dual enrollment, accelerated programs, and standard community college courses.

Faculty Members' Perceptions of Rigor in Dual Enrollment, Accelerated Programs, and Standard Community College Courses

Colin Ferguson, Pete Baker, Dana Burnett

Presumably, high school students in dual enrollment courses can earn up to the equivalent of two years of postsecondary credits prior to graduating from high school. But what if dual enrollment courses are not equivalent to similar courses offered on the college campus? If dual enrollment course rigor is not on par with that of traditional college courses, the less rigorous dual enrollment courses, while representing an opportunity for significant cost savings, could put students at a distinct disadvantage, rendering these students less likely to succeed in traditional college courses and, hence, less likely to complete a four-year degree. A significant portion of dual enrollment coursework is offered at the high school campus by high school faculty who have adjunct status at the community college. Concerns about the quality and equivalency of dual enrollment courses have been raised since these courses' inception.

Carol Dougan (2005), who has served as a community college faculty member, dean, and vice president, described what she believed were fundamental problems when assessing the efficacy of dual enrollment courses:

> In my 15 years of teaching in the arts and in business, many high-school-age students attended my classes. Rarely did their work approach the quality or reveal the level of understanding that I expected of my students. It seemed to me that students with little life experience and maturity dragged down the level of discourse in my college classes ... faculty members told me of their struggle to maintain quality and integrity in their dual enrollment classes. (p. B20)

NEW DIRECTIONS FOR COMMUNITY COLLEGES, no. 169, Spring 2015 © 2015 Wiley Periodicals, Inc.
Published online in Wiley Online Library (wileyonlinelibrary.com) • DOI: 10.1002/cc.20135

How do faculty members perceive the level of rigor of dual enrollment courses compared to similar community college courses offered in the first two years of college? The context for the research was a small, public community college in the Southern United States, which we will call Townsville Community College (TCC). This qualitative study compared the perceptions of course rigor among three faculty groups: qualified high school faculty teaching dual enrollment at the high school, college faculty teaching dual enrolled students on the community college campus, and college faculty teaching standard community college students on the community college campus. We operationalized course rigor in two ways. First, we examined how grades were comprised through an analysis of the grading requirements based on course syllabi, which reflect faculty instructional and pedagogical philosophies. Second, we conducted interviews with faculty members to understand students' nonacademic behaviors, attitudes, and dispositions. Faculty perceptions of students' behaviors and dispositions provide insight into faculty expectations for college courses and college students. In turn, faculty expectations are an important dimension of course rigor in that they shape the extent to which the course environment is at the collegiate level.

Programmatic Descriptions

At TCC, *dual enrollment* courses enroll students who have not yet graduated from high school and consist of classes designed for college transfer, which are taught on a high school or community college campus. Dually enrolled students usually receive academic credit for their work from both the high school and the community college. Students in dual enrollment courses enroll in these courses in an à la carte fashion, so dual enrollment does not represent a "program," per se. Instead, dual enrollment can be understood simply as a suite of courses in which students choose to enroll. The *accelerated program*, on the other hand, represents a more prescriptive program within TCC's larger dual enrollment system. Students participating in TCC's accelerated program enroll in courses designed for college transfer that are part of a defined general studies program. In addition to courses taken at their individual high school sites, accelerated program students attend classes on TCC's campus, taking a minimum of four and a maximum of ten courses on the college campus throughout their junior and senior years of high school. Students who successfully complete the program are awarded an associate's degree in either general education or science concurrently with their high school diploma. For the purpose of this study, students who are enrolled in classes at a community college, but who are not enrolled in either dual enrollment or accelerated program classes, and are high school graduates are designated as *standard* community college students.

Faculty

Faculty members who participated in this study represented three faculty subgroups summarized in Table 8.1: (1) high school faculty teaching dual enrollment courses at the high school sites, (2) TCC faculty teaching students enrolled in the college's accelerated program, and (3) TCC faculty teaching standard community college students in general studies courses. The general studies courses taught by this third faculty subgroup are among those courses that are also included in TCC's accelerated program. Faculty who teach these courses for standard community college students were selected in order for the researchers to ensure that comparisons between courses were fair (i.e., to ensure that the rigor of a lower level course would not be compared to that of an upper level course). While the faculty members who teach dual enrollment courses at the high school sites (i.e., group 1) do not teach standard community college students, each of the other faculty subgroups teach both dual enrolled and standard community college students, providing the basis for the comparisons examined in this study.

Faculty Teaching Dual Enrollment Courses at the High School Sites. The five high school faculty members who taught dual enrollment at the high school had an average of 24 years' experience in the classroom that ranged from 13 to 35 years. Two of the faculty members reported that they had the necessary requirements to retire, but stated that they had no intention of retiring. In fact the faculty member with 35 years of service stated, "I have the best course load and student population in the school, as long as I keep teaching these classes I have no reason to retire anytime soon." Within this subgroup, one participating faculty member taught English literature, while another taught U.S. history. The three remaining faculty taught precalculus, calculus, and biology, respectively.

Faculty Teaching Accelerated Program Courses on the TCC Campus. The five college faculty members teaching accelerated program students had an average of 17 years' experience in the classroom that ranged from 7 to 27 years. One of the five faculty members from this group had a significant amount of experience teaching in the high school setting, having begun her teaching career at the high school. Within this subgroup, two participants

Table 8.1   Participating Faculty Subgroups

	Subgroup 1	Subgroup 2	Subgroup 3
Number of faculty	5	5	5

Subgroup 1: Faculty teaching dual enrollment courses at the high school sites.
Subgroup 2: Faculty teaching accelerated program courses on the TCC campus.
Subgroup 3: Faculty teaching standard courses on the TCC campus.

taught information technology, one taught music, one taught speech, and the final participant taught psychology.

Faculty Teaching Standard Courses on the TCC Campus.   The five community college faculty selected for participation were chosen on the basis of their instruction of courses that are currently offered for dual enrollment at the high school. This group had an average of 16 years' experience that ranged from 11 to 27 years. Included in this group were two faculty members who began their teaching careers as high school faculty members. Closely mirroring the high school faculty, one teacher taught precalculus, one taught calculus, one taught U.S. history, one taught English literature, and the final participant within this subgroup taught speech.

Methods and Procedures

The data for this study are based on analyses of participating faculty members' course syllabi as well as semistructured interviews conducted with the 15 high school and college faculty members described earlier. The interview protocol consisted of a series of questions that focused on grading policies and practices including the number of tests, weight of assignments, and other less traditionally academic, often affective means through which faculty members engaged in the holistic evaluation of their students (e.g., maturity, study habits, etc.). This protocol assisted in guiding the interviews and ensuring that the questioning of each participant was consistent. Participants' responses were analyzed for themes within, among, and between the subgroups of faculty participants. After each interview was completed, the researchers completed an interview comparison process. This process allowed the researchers to identify themes from the interviews where specific comments and information can be recorded and organized. The original themes were developed from prepared questions asked to each faculty member. Additional themes were added on the basis of the follow-up questions or information provided by the respondents.

Findings

Findings presented in this section consisted of two major sections: (a) components of the final grade based on analysis of course syllabi and pertinent interview responses, and (b) faculty members' comparisons of students enrolled in dual enrollment courses to students not enrolled in dual enrollment courses. These two sections are presented in subsections, each focusing on one of the subgroups of participating faculty members.

Components of the Final Grade.   Data from the analysis of participating faculty members' syllabi as well as interview data provided insights into the nature and variety of graded assignments and how those assignments impact the calculation of the final grade. Likewise, the number, type, and relative value of assignments that were utilized during the semester varied.

Faculty Teaching Dual Enrollment Courses at the High School Sites. The components utilized to calculate the final course grade for dual enrollment students varied widely, ranging from 0% to 60% of the grade derived from tests. The sole consistency within this group was the requirement that the course consist of multiple types of assignments, selected by the instructor, from tests, projects, writing assignments, homework, or labs for science-related courses. The types of assignments varied, but all high school faculty members reported at least one assignment "of significance" each week. One faculty member complained about the number and variety of assignments given to students, saying, "I am required to give different types of assignments [to dual enrollment students] by the [high] school administration in order to show I am offering instruction that is differentiated from that provided to high school students [not enrolled in dual enrollment courses]." This indicated that dual enrollment high school teachers did not have autonomy in determining how the final grade is calculated.

There was clear agreement among the high school faculty that the dual enrollment courses taught at the high school were at least if not more rigorous than community college courses taught on campus. One faculty member stated, "My class is harder than the community college classes. I have former students tell me my class was harder than classes they took at the university." The high school faculty reported that they ensure the rigor of their courses by working with other faculty members from both the high school and the community college, comparing their courses to the national Advanced Placement curriculum and examining the final grades.

Faculty Teaching Accelerated Program Courses on the TCC Campus. The college faculty who taught accelerated program students varied in the number and types of assignments from which they derived the final grade. This group reported that tests accounted for 0–75% of the final course grade. Each course in this group included a writing assignment. The relative weight for the writing assignment varied from 25% to 100% of the final course grade. Several faculty members reported that course content often dictated how assignments formed the final grades. Several faculty members commented that multiple types of assignments were combined and were inseparable when determining grades. Examples of this include research, writing, and presentation grades, which were inseparable from project grades. Three of these faculty members reported utilizing the same syllabi in their standard college courses as a way of ensuring rigor, while two other faculty members reported that they utilized their experience in the classroom as a way to ensure the rigor of the course. Two faculty from this group felt that their courses were more rigorous than similar general education courses taught on the college campus. Three faculty members specifically stated that they utilized the same syllabi, textbooks, and assignments for their dual enrollment course as for their courses taken by standard community college students.

NEW DIRECTIONS FOR COMMUNITY COLLEGES • DOI: 10.1002/cc

Faculty Teaching Standard Courses on the TCC Campus.   The college faculty who taught general education courses to standard community college students reported that tests accounted for 0–100% of final course grades. The calculation of the final grade for one course included only essays written for the course. This group of instructors was inconsistent in the number and type of assignments used in the calculation of the final grade. One of the faculty members commented that "as a new faculty member I provided students with a greater number of assignments at first, and as I gained more experience the number of assignments decreased." Another faculty member stated, "When I gave more assignments I was grading all the time, and it allowed students to make good grades even when they didn't do well on the tests." Faculty had the freedom to design a course that effectively reflects their educational philosophies; however, this freedom yielded inconsistency and uncontrolled confounding variables when course-level comparisons are made.

Although the type and number of assignments varied, community college faculty interviewed for this study appear to make no differentiation between standard and dual enrollment students when designing their courses. Similarly, these faculty who also teach dual enrollment courses on the high school campuses work with other faculty members, often from the community college, to create courses designed to mirror the structural rigor of community college courses.

Faculty Members' Comparisons of Students Enrolled in Dual Enrollment Courses to Standard High School and Community College Students. Participating faculty members were asked to compare their dual enrolled students to other students in their courses. Since high school faculty members lacked the ability to compare their dual enrolled students to other standard community college students by virtue of the fact that these faculty members worked exclusively at the high school sites, this subgroup of participants was able to compare their dual enrolled students to high school students not participating in dual enrollment. In all other cases, comparisons presented next are between dual enrolled community college students and their standard community college peers.

Faculty Teaching Dual Enrollment Courses at the High School Sites. Among high school faculty, all participants reported that the dual enrolled students achieved at higher levels, thought more critically, and engaged in more effective learning behaviors than high school students not participating in dual enrollment. These faculty cited dual enrolled students' strong work ethic and time management skills. One faculty member noted, "The dual enrollment students are normally in multiple dual enrollment courses and have better time management skills and expect to make higher grades when compared to students not enrolled in dual enrollment general education courses." The high school faculty participants reported that dual enrollment helped students prepare for the academic rigors of college; however, three of these high school faculty members teaching dual enrolled students questioned the extent to which the dual enrolled students' maturity would allow them to thrive in college or university settings.

Faculty Teaching Accelerated Program Courses on the TCC Campus. Among college faculty teaching accelerated program students, three reported that this subset of dual enrolled students was similar in academic ability when compared to community college students taking identical general education courses. Three faculty members within this subgroup concluded that dual enrollment courses allowed students to understand college expectations. One faculty member remarked, "Dual enrollment students were developing the study habits that would help them succeed in college."

One faculty member stated that "students were academically prepared and some were extremely gifted; however, their emotional maturity was not on level with other college students. They bring a lot of drama to class." Other faculty members who were interviewed were also concerned about dual enrolled students' maturity level. When students in dual enrollment courses encountered problems with courses or with faculty, they were less likely to take initiative and address the problem. One faculty member stated, "In all the years I have taught in the accelerated program, I have never had a student meet with me during office hours, and I meet with my other community college students all the time." Thus, faculty perceived that dual enrollment students were not acting and behaving in ways that college students should to be successful in college.

Faculty Teaching Standard Courses on the TCC Campus. Of the five college faculty teaching standard community college students, only three could identify former dual enrolled students. These three reported that former dual enrolled students who were currently enrolled at TCC performed as well as or better than their standard community college students.

Summary of Findings

As a result of the analysis of syllabi and interviews with faculty who teach students enrolled in dual enrollment courses at high school sites, those who teach accelerated program students at the TCC campus, and faculty who teach standard students at TCC, we draw three conclusions.

1. Based on the analysis of course syllabi and faculty interviews, dual enrollment general education courses were at least as rigorous if not more rigorous than general education courses taught to standard students on the community college campus. Although the design and content of a course varied with the instructor, the course rigor and quality did not vary in relation to the type of student enrolled.
2. Faculty tended to assess the academic ability of accelerated program students and students enrolled in dual enrollment courses as generally higher than standard students. This held for comparisons between

dual enrolled and standard students at both the high school and community college.

3. Faculty perceived that students in dual enrollment courses did not behave like college students and were less mature than their older, standard community college students. Whereas the academic "college readiness" of these students may be adequate, their affective readiness to participate in college courses two years before high school graduation may present challenges that could require significant support.

Implications

Comprehensive evaluation of dual enrollment programs is important for community college leaders to initiate. The need for evaluation will only escalate as dual enrollment courses expand and open their doors to students with more diverse academic backgrounds. Although dual enrollment programs have many tangible benefits such as saving students money, it is imperative that they are of high quality and adequately prepare students to succeed in colleges and universities. In order to determine the extent to which dual enrollment programming is fulfilling this part of its mission, community colleges can systematically compare the rigor of dual enrollment courses and standard, non–dual enrollment college courses to ensure students experience college-level work. Critical to this evaluation process are faculty members' voices whose perspectives on course equivalency and relative rigor are guided by their pedagogical knowledge and understanding of the students they teach. Specifically, faculty members should explore their academic and nonacademic expectations of their students. As this study demonstrated, although dual enrollment students are often highly capable academically, they may lag behind their traditionally college-aged peers in terms of maturity and other behaviors and dispositions expected of college students. This disjuncture, if left unexplored, could lead faculty to make decisions about their courses that may not meet their students' holistic developmental needs.

Equivalent Course Content.   Some may wonder whether it is necessary or even desirable to ensure equivalency between dual enrollment and traditional college courses. After all, variability in terms of rigor and content exists among college courses. Some college courses are more difficult than others. Still, when viewed in their totality, the average rigor of college courses should be higher than the average rigor of high school courses. If a student receives college credit for completing courses with levels of rigor more characteristic of the average high school class, that student may struggle when they transition to college-level courses, which is a disservice to students. Perhaps course-to-course equivalence is less important than holistic, programmatic equivalence between dual enrollment programs and traditional college programs.

New Directions for Community Colleges • DOI: 10.1002/cc

To ensure that the quality and rigor of dual enrollment courses are, when viewed holistically, equivalent to courses offered at the college level, participating school districts and community colleges across the nation could form advisory boards to review course content and provide any resulting recommendations. Advisory board members should be drawn from faculty members who teach dual enrollment courses and administrative representatives from participating high schools and community colleges. The National Alliance for Concurrent Enrollment Partnerships (NACEP) provides a standards-based model for dual enrollment assessment and evaluation that includes, among other things, training, regular assessment, and professional development among college and high school faculty to ensure the quality of dual enrollment courses. Although this model, which is featured in Chapter 9 of this volume, does not directly evaluate dual enrollment courses relative to non–dual enrollment courses, it is an alternative mechanism for ensuring course rigor.

Support Services.   Based on the results of this research, support services for students who enroll in dual enrollment courses taught at high schools and community colleges may be necessary to nurture the development of students' affective and nonacademic skills and behaviors. Examples of support services that could be provided to students include a specialized orientation program, academic advising, career counseling, and possibly tutoring. In addition to satisfying accrediting agency requirements, specialized orientations, advising, career counseling, and tutoring designed to meet the unique needs of dual enrolled students can help ensure their academic success in dual enrollment courses and as they transition to college. The delivery of these services may not be accessible to students due to structural and organizational issues and factors. For example, even if the college has effective programs to support students, if faculty members and support labs are inaccessible during hours that are convenient for all dual enrollment students, students may not benefit from these services.

Reference

Dougan, C. (2005). The pitfalls of college courses for high-school students. *Chronicle of Higher Education, 52*(10), B20.

COLIN FERGUSON *is the accelerated career pathway coordinator at Patrick Henry Community College.*

PETE BAKER *is a lecturer in the Department of Teaching & Learning within Old Dominion University's Darden College of Education.*

DANA BURNETT *is a professor of practice in the Department of Educational Foundations & Leadership within Old Dominion University's Darden College of Education.*

9

This chapter describes how implementing the National Alliance of Concurrent Enrollment Partnerships' 17 accreditation standards strengthens a concurrent enrollment program, enhances secondary–postsecondary relations, and benefits students, their families, and secondary and postsecondary institutions.

Strengthening Concurrent Enrollment Through NACEP Accreditation

Kent Scheffel, Yvette McLemore, Adam Lowe

Concurrent enrollment, known as dual credit in Illinois, has played a key role in Lewis and Clark Community College achieving the longest continuous growth trend in Illinois. The college experienced its 18th consecutive fall semester enrollment increase in 2013, establishing a record high enrollment of 8,520 students. While Lewis and Clark's overall enrollment stood at 8,179 in 2009 and grew 4.1% by 2013, concurrent enrollment at the college grew 36.8% during the same period and increased from 2,137 in fall 2009 to 2,923 in fall 2013. The growth has resulted in the college's concurrent enrollment program being one of the largest in Illinois. In 1996, 442 students earned 5,849 concurrent enrollment credit hours. The annual number of credit hours grew to 29,182 in 2012–2013, averaging 6.7 credit hours per student. Courses are offered to students at no charge at the 16 public and two private high schools in the college district, and, based on Lewis and Clark's tuition rates, students and their families have saved more than $26 million since fall 1996.

History

Like many colleges around the country, Lewis and Clark's credit in escrow program was an articulated credit system that grew under Tech Prep in the late 1980s to enable students to continue on their chosen course of study without needing to duplicate coursework after matriculating to Lewis and Clark. As documented by researchers at the University of Illinois (Bragg, 2001), students did not fully benefit from these articulated credits as they were often unaware that they had accumulated college credit, lacked

NEW DIRECTIONS FOR COMMUNITY COLLEGES, no. 169, Spring 2015 © 2015 Wiley Periodicals, Inc.
Published online in Wiley Online Library (wileyonlinelibrary.com) • DOI: 10.1002/cc.20136

confidence that their high school classes had sufficiently prepared them for more advanced courses, and received credit only if they enrolled in a specific degree program at Lewis and Clark and succeeded in subsequent courses in that program of study.

Building on the experience with credit in escrow, Lewis and Clark strengthened its offerings when it converted to concurrent enrollment by credentialing high school instructors to offer the college's courses in the high schools. This conversion enabled a student to earn transcripted college credit at the time the student successfully completed the course and broadened the program to include academic courses. During this period of transition and growth, the college recognized the need to establish systems to ensure that it maintained sufficient control over the credentials of high school instructors, the curriculum, and the methods of assessment. The National Alliance of Concurrent Enrollment Partnerships (NACEP) accreditation standards (NACEP, 2012) provided a blueprint for the college to enhance its quality and operation.

NACEP was founded in 1999 by some of the nation's oldest and most prominent concurrent enrollment partnerships during a period of rapid growth both in the number of programs and participating students. A key concern of the leaders who established NACEP was the quality of college classes offered to high school students by concurrent enrollment partnerships, and they shared a common belief that institutions of higher education should follow best practices to ensure the quality of college classes taught by high school teachers. In 2002, NACEP adopted national standards, and in 2004, the first four concurrent enrollment programs were accredited after a team of peers carefully reviewed documentation on how each program met NACEP's standards. Lewis and Clark began working on its NACEP accreditation application in 2005 and was awarded accreditation in 2007. The program was one of the first 25 in the United States to earn accreditation and continued to be the only accredited program in Illinois at the time of Lewis and Clark's successful reaccreditation in 2014. As of May 2014, there were 92 concurrent enrollment partnerships nationwide that hold NACEP accreditation. NACEP's accreditation standards cover the areas of curriculum, faculty, students, assessment, and program evaluation, and promote policies and practices to ensure that college courses offered in the high school are consistent with the courses offered on campus at the sponsoring college or university.[1]

Implementing the NACEP Standards at Lewis and Clark

This section outlines the process of implementing the NACEP standards as they apply to the following five areas: curriculum, faculty, students, assessment, and evaluation.

Curriculum.   While accreditation has proven valuable, implementation of the standards created challenges and concerns at the college and

NEW DIRECTIONS FOR COMMUNITY COLLEGES • DOI: 10.1002/cc

high schools. The curriculum standards focus on ensuring that concurrent enrollment courses feature the same curriculum as taught on campus, with high school visits by postsecondary faculty to ensure alignment. Challenges in implementing the standards include identifying college faculty who are interested in working with their high school counterparts; ongoing collaboration between instructors to ensure that courses reflect the pedagogical, theoretical, and philosophical orientation of the specific academic department of the college; and the willingness of high school faculty to alter their curriculum and undergo a review by college faculty.

Faculty.   The faculty standards require college approval of high school instructors and discipline-specific training and orientation prior to teaching a concurrent enrollment course, annual discipline-specific professional development, and procedures for addressing instructors who fail to comply with the college's expectations. It is common for high school administrators to be frustrated by the college's decisions on who can teach concurrent enrollment. While instructors may produce positive outcomes in their classrooms, they may not have the necessary credentials to teach for the college. Postsecondary institutions can become frustrated with the cost and faculty hours necessary to provide discipline-specific training and ongoing professional development. Instructors who fail to comply with the college's expectations, and the need to remove these instructors from concurrent enrollment courses, create a challenge for both the high school and college.

Students.   Standards related to student selection and registration can prove challenging for the college but are critical so that students fully benefit from their early experience with college. The standards focus on officially registering students, ensuring students meet course prerequisites, and informing students and secondary schools of their rights and responsibilities. Conducting placement testing, reviewing for prerequisite courses, and enrolling large numbers of high school students create logistical issues. College personnel visit individual high schools and conduct placement testing in computer labs. Any prerequisite requirements are then reviewed and eligible students are registered by Lewis and Clark staff. The process can become labor intensive and time consuming for the college, and high schools prefer to see the process completed as quickly as possible to keep lost instructional time to a minimum. The alternative is to have high school students come to the campus for placement testing and enrollment. However, that practice results in a greater amount of lost instructional time or evening or weekend staff hours.

Informing students of their rights and responsibilities related to enrollment results in additional work for staff as well. The college sends letters to students and their parents, and policies and guidelines are included in information sent to the high schools and are available in the student handbook. Families, school districts, and the college benefit in the long run if students and parents understand the impact of registering for a transcribed

NEW DIRECTIONS FOR COMMUNITY COLLEGES • DOI: 10.1002/cc

college course, and the importance of withdrawing from the course if the student is not making satisfactory progress.

Assessment.   Assessment and learning outcome standards help to ensure that high school students are evaluated in the same fashion as students receiving the instruction on campus. The standards focus on holding high school and college students to the same academic standards of achievement and ensuring that both groups are assessed with the same degree of rigor and methods. Lewis and Clark's academic program coordinators have diligently tracked student outcomes and success.

For example, the coordinator for English and literature uses matrices to track the outcomes of concurrent enrollment students in comparison to on-campus students. She ensures consistency in assignments and grading by requiring the same writing assignments for both groups of students, with college and high school faculty collaborating on the grading to ensure that they are evaluating students in a similar manner.

Several courses require common assessments that are prepared by on-campus faculty. The assessments aid in the requirement to cover the same course content and assist in determining whether concurrent enrollment and college students are achieving at comparable levels. In programs such as Computer-Aided Design (CAD) Drafting and Computer Graphics and Design, students are required to complete identical projects. The college and high school courses use the same software, which enables Lewis and Clark faculty to determine whether concurrent enrollment students understand the material and are able to implement various design features within the software. The corresponding projects also aid in determining whether grading is aligned.

Evaluation.   Standards related to program evaluation aid the college in understanding the overall viability and success of the program. NACEP's guidelines call for end-of-term student course evaluations, a survey of concurrent enrollment alumni who have been out of high school for one year, a survey of alumni four years after graduation from high school, and a survey of high school instructors, principals, and guidance counselors.

The end-of-term evaluations create multiple challenges. Lewis and Clark offers approximately 600 concurrent enrollment course sections annually. While the evaluations are completed online through Scantron's Course Climate system, it is still necessary to disseminate the results to more than 130 instructors in 18 high schools. The academic program coordinators at Lewis and Clark review the surveys, and teachers are informed when the surveys are available. For courses offered in computer labs, completing the evaluation is relatively easy, but the completion process is more difficult for courses taught in a traditional classroom. Students must be reminded to complete the survey while outside of class. Some students are very responsive in completing the evaluation, while others receive several reminders and still fail to respond. Receiving feedback from students can prove very valuable in the college's ongoing efforts to strengthen the concurrent enrollment program. However, the logistics involved in coordinating and distributing the evaluations with a limited staff is a hurdle.

NACEP standards require surveying concurrent enrollment students one year and four years after high school graduation, and surveying former concurrent enrollment students presents both unique challenges and opportunities. Obtaining a satisfactory response rate is a concern due to frequent changes in the contact information of high school graduates.

Surveying students who are enrolled in or have graduated from a postsecondary institution can provide valuable feedback. These students have had the opportunity to experience whether and how concurrent enrollment was beneficial to their postsecondary education. We have found that many students saw the value of concurrent enrollment after one year, and the students appreciate earning college credit even more four years after graduation. At this later date, students have had the opportunity to evaluate whether their concurrent enrollment courses have saved them time, money, or both. They are also able to reflect on whether concurrent enrollment courses helped better prepare them for college. Among the most recent four-year survey results, 92% of the respondents rated their overall satisfaction with the concurrent enrollment program as either excellent or good, 72% strongly agreed or agreed that they were better prepared academically for college, and 100% stated that they would recommend concurrent enrollment courses to their peers.

Feedback from secondary instructors, principals, and guidance counselors is also a valuable tool in measuring the effectiveness of the program. These individuals are in daily contact with the concurrent enrollment students and witness the program's strengths and opportunities for improvement. Responses from high school personnel are reviewed by the college and appropriate steps are taken if needed. It is the college's goal to make sure that the concurrent enrollment classes continue to function as a high-quality program.

Accreditation Benefits and Challenges

This section details the benefits of NACEP accreditation to four stakeholders: students, secondary schools, instructors, and the college. It also presents the challenges encountered by each of these stakeholders.

Benefits to Students.   NACEP accreditation signals to students that the concurrent enrollment instruction and learning outcomes they experience are comparable to college courses on the college campus. Common syllabi and assessments, professional development, and site visits to the high schools are critical components in ensuring a high-quality learning experience. The rigorous curriculum also proves beneficial to students when they enter a postsecondary institution. They have a better understanding of what is expected in a college course and are better prepared to make the necessary commitment to achieve success.

For many students, experiencing the expectations of college coursework while in high school aids in the transition to their postsecondary career, allowing them to envision themselves as college goers and practice the role of being a college student, with research showing that it can change students' beliefs about their ability to succeed in college (Karp, 2012). However, the benefits of concurrent enrollment are unlikely to be fully realized unless programs implement practices to ensure the authenticity of the college courses and experiences (Borden, Taylor, Park, & Seiler, 2013; Karp 2012). Many new community college and university students can be overwhelmed with living on their own, adapting to the freedoms that come with college, and adjusting to more rigorous courses. Experiencing the rigor prior to exposure to other aspects of college life lessens the adjustment for students.

Transcribing the grades earned through concurrent enrollment aids students as they enroll in various postsecondary institutions. A national study of chief academic officers at 540 colleges and universities found that 92% of public postsecondary institutions award credit for transcribed dual and concurrent courses, similar to the rate of awarding credit for student performance on Advanced Placement exams (91%) and significantly higher than for International Baccalaureate exams (40%). Only 78% of private institutions accepted dual and concurrent enrollment credit, consistent with the lower rates of awarding credit by these institutions for transfer students (Western Interstate Commission for Higher Education, 2006). For a few years, the University of Illinois placed added restrictions on the transfer of certain concurrent enrollment courses due to a perception that the community colleges issuing concurrent enrollment were not upholding the academic integrity of the courses. To regain the university's trust, the Illinois Community College System demonstrated that its administrative rules—based on NACEP's standards—mandated that colleges impose effective academic controls and the system office provided sufficient oversight of the implementation of those rules. Similarly, university systems in Minnesota and South Dakota have recognized NACEP's standards and accreditation, enacting policies that require public colleges and universities to award transfer credit for concurrent enrollment offered by an NACEP-accredited program (South Dakota Board of Regents, 2010; State of Minnesota, 2005). Reflecting states' concerns that their investment in concurrent enrollment is well spent and that students benefit from high rates of credit transfer, NACEP's standards serve as a model for statewide quality standards in 16 states. State policies in nine of these states additionally require, provide incentives, or encourage colleges to obtain NACEP accreditation (NACEP, 2014).

Benefits to Secondary Schools.   Critics of concurrent enrollment contend that college rigor and learning outcomes are not necessarily achieved in courses offered in high schools. NACEP accreditation provides school district administrators and faculty with the assurance that students are receiving a learning experience that corresponds to on-campus classes.

Adherence to the NACEP standards also enables district personnel to express confidence in the program, resulting in parental support and a positive public perception of concurrent enrollment.

The close relationships with the high schools have led to Lewis and Clark providing the newest software in high school computer labs, including the newest versions of Microsoft operating systems and Office, as well as CAD, web design, and computer graphics software. The ongoing software updates help ensure that high school students receive the same software training as on-campus students. Close collaboration with the high schools has also resulted in high school students coming to the campus and earning Certified Nursing Assistant (CNA) certificates. The certification enables students to begin working as a CNA immediately following their high school graduation.

Benefits to Instructors. Teachers recognize the value of accreditation through the professional development that is required by NACEP accreditation. High school teachers were initially apprehensive when they learned that they would be required to take part in professional development on an annual basis. Some teachers were also concerned about Lewis and Clark being involved with decisions about instruction in the high school. However, most teachers now appreciate the professional development and understand the need for Lewis and Clark's curricular oversight of its courses. Many districts have made cuts to their professional development budgets and generally focus on pedagogy rather than continued discipline-specific training. The sessions offered at the college are an opportunity to meet with college faculty in the shared discipline and colleagues teaching the same courses in other schools to share ideas and gain information that aids student instruction. A majority of high school teachers now look forward to the meetings and value the time spent at the college. They also receive professional development credits that apply toward their recertification.

Another benefit of the professional development is the collaboration that occurs between the high school and college faculty. The instructors work together to align curriculum and evaluate outcomes, enabling high school instructors to learn college expectations from college faculty in their discipline and observe firsthand the skills that students need to succeed in college courses. Conversely, college faculty have become better informed about the specific skills and content knowledge their students are taught during high school. This collaboration is critical to overcome the gap in perceptions regarding college readiness. While 89% of high school teachers nationwide report that students are well prepared for college-level work in their content area, only 26% of college faculty agree with that statement (ACT, Inc., 2013).

Benefits to the College. NACEP accreditation has proven to be valuable to Lewis and Clark. Approximately 33% of the high school graduates in the Lewis and Clark district enroll at the college. However, 40% of the students who participate in concurrent enrollment or in the Early Start program, which enables seniors to enroll in two courses on campus at half the normal cost, matriculate at Lewis and Clark following their high school graduation. Since 2007, an average of 70% of all new enrollees at Lewis and Clark have concurrent enrollment credit. Students and parents involved with concurrent enrollment gain an understanding of how accreditation has been beneficial. Their understanding and their appreciation of the quality education offered at Lewis and Clark have been rewarded by an increased percentage of concurrent enrollment students enrolling at the college.

While Lewis and Clark has always enjoyed a strong relationship with its high schools, NACEP accreditation has helped strengthen the relationships. Districts now view concurrent enrollment as an important part of their curriculum and take steps to enhance the program in the same way they work to enhance other elements within the district. For example, it is common for high schools to contact Lewis and Clark prior to making hiring decisions that could impact concurrent enrollment offerings. Districts have narrowed the field of potential candidates for a teaching position and have then contacted Lewis and Clark to determine which, if any, of the remaining candidates have the appropriate credentials to teach concurrent enrollment courses.

When new teachers have questions or become hesitant regarding curriculum alignment or learning outcomes, the accreditation standards aid in demonstrating the reasoning for various actions. The standards are clear on what actions are necessary and thus it becomes clear to the teacher that the district and college are working together on all concurrent enrollment courses, and the instructor soon realizes the expectations for a concurrent enrollment course.

An unexpected benefit to Lewis and Clark came recently when the college began preparing for institutional reaccreditation by the Higher Learning Commission (HLC). In 2012, the Commission adopted revised *Criteria for Accreditation* (HLC, 2012) that explicitly established standards related to concurrent enrollment for the first time. These minimum standards will raise the expectations for many concurrent enrollment programs across the HLC region now that site review teams have begun to specifically ask questions about concurrent enrollment programs. For Lewis and Clark, however, our adherence to the more extensive NACEP standards meant the college was already meeting HLC's concurrent enrollment requirements and had the documentation necessary to demonstrate this to peer reviewers during the site visit.

The close collaboration with the school districts that is a part of accreditation has also resulted in other programs and activities that have benefited the college and students. A unique aspect of our work with school districts is the Silver Medallion Banquet. The top 8% of seniors at all high schools in the college district are recognized at the banquet that is sponsored by Lewis and Clark, the local newspaper, and area businesses, with the event being held at the college. The newspaper prints a supplement that includes a photo of each recipient, and each student is recognized individually at the event. Many of the districts now make note of Silver Medallion recipients at their graduation ceremonies.

Challenges.   The primary challenges the college continues to encounter associated with NACEP accreditation are related to faculty and budgets. The faculty obstacles take multiple forms and can occur at both Lewis and Clark and the high schools. When the college is initially developing course partnerships within a discipline, or when a new program coordinator assumes responsibility for an academic program, the coordinator at times is reluctant to support NACEP's standards. A new coordinator often faces many time demands and feels a site visit to a high school is something that can be delayed or ignored. At times it is necessary for the appropriate dean to become involved and point out the importance of site visits. As the program has grown, so has the importance of college staff who coordinate and monitor the faculty's role in professional development and curricular oversight. Lewis and Clark as an institution needs to ensure consistent faculty oversight over academic matters across all courses taught in all disciplines and not allow this academic oversight to fall by the wayside due to changes in faculty coordinators.

From a high school standpoint, budget constraints make it difficult for school districts to hire faculty with the required credentials. These constraints can also lead some teachers to feel overwhelmed when they are required to accomplish more in the same amount of time and can result in reluctance to attend professional development activities. After attending the professional development sessions, new teachers join veteran instructors in placing value on the training sessions. Budgets become an issue as well in meeting curriculum requirements. School districts frequently struggle to provide the textbooks and software that are necessary for concurrent enrollment courses.

Summary

Students and parents realize that high-quality instruction is provided and transcribed, and the credit will transfer to two- or four-year institutions and result in a more successful postsecondary career. High school instructors and administrators understand the importance of accreditation and the fact that it helps drive quality into the concurrent enrollment program. For other postsecondary institutions, NACEP accreditation is a signal that Lewis and Clark treats concurrent enrollment in a serious manner and focuses on college learning outcomes, thereby providing transfer students with the knowledge they need to be successful. Lewis and Clark benefits through an enhanced public image, a strong program that has led to increased enrollment, and the assurance that students in the program are receiving true college courses and outcomes. The accreditation has also increased the concurrent enrollment program's on-campus stature. It is recognized with other accredited programs at the college such as Nursing and Dental Hygiene, resulting in additional administrative support and more respect on campus.

Note

1. The standards can be found at www.nacep.org/accreditation/standards

References

ACT, Inc. (2013). *National curriculum survey 2012: Policy implications on preparing for higher standards*. Iowa City, IA: Author.

Borden, V., Taylor, J., Park, E., & Seiler, D. (2013). *Dual credit in U.S. higher education: A study of state policy and quality assurance practices*. Chicago, IL: The Higher Learning Commission of the North Central Association.

Bragg, D. (2001). *Promising outcomes for Tech Prep participants in eight local consortia: A summary of initial results*. Columbus, OH: National Research Center for Career and Technical Education.

Higher Learning Commission (HLC). (2012). *Criteria for accreditation*. Chicago, IL: Author.

Karp, M. M. (2012). "I don't know, I've never been to college!" Dual enrollment as a college readiness strategy. In E. Hofmann & D. Voloch (Eds.), *New Directions for Higher Education: No. 158. Dual enrollment: Strategies, outcomes, and lessons for school–college partnerships* (pp. 21–28). San Francisco, CA: Jossey-Bass. doi:10.1002/he.20011

National Alliance of Concurrent Enrollment Partnerships (NACEP). (2012). *National concurrent enrollment partnership standards*. Chapel Hill, NC: Author.

National Alliance of Concurrent Enrollment Partnerships (NACEP). (2014). *NACEP in state policy*. Chapel Hill, NC: Author. Retrieved from http://www.nacep.org/research-policy/legislation-policy/

South Dakota Board of Regents. (2010). *"Section 2:5 transfer of credit" in policy manual*. Pierre, SD: Author.

State of Minnesota. (2005). *"124D.09 postsecondary enrollment options act, subdivision 12. Credits" in Minnesota statutes*. St. Paul, MN: Office of the Revisor of Statutes, State of Minnesota.

Western Interstate Commission for Higher Education. (2006). *Accelerated learning options: Moving the needle on access and success*. Boulder, CO: Author.

KENT SCHEFFEL *serves as vice president of enrollment services at Lewis & Clark Community College.*

YVETTE MCLEMORE *is the director of High School Partnerships & Community Education Centers at Lewis & Clark Community College.*

ADAM LOWE *serves as executive director of the National Alliance of Concurrent Enrollment Partnerships (NACEP).*

10

This chapter contextualizes and extends the previous chapters by addressing the intertwined issues of structural systems reform and college completion, as well as the role dual enrollment can play in ensuring equitable postsecondary outcomes for underrepresented students.

Dual Enrollment, Structural Reform, and the Completion Agenda

Melinda Mechur Karp

The chapters in this volume have explored dual enrollment from the perspective of students, staff, faculty, and institutions. They present a compelling picture of a program that, for all its challenges, can positively influence educational outcomes. In some ways, however, they present a picture of a static, stand-alone initiative in which discrete partnerships of colleges and high schools work together to meet the needs of their particular students.

Dual enrollment can and should be located in the broader context of national efforts to reform postsecondary education, however. In this chapter, I argue that the promising institution- and state-level findings presented in this volume indicate that dual enrollment is a strategy that, if sufficiently leveraged, can help meet the nation's postsecondary completion goals. By strategically linking high schools and colleges and requiring these two types of institutions to change how they operate, dual enrollment requires educators and policymakers to rethink how they structure and deliver education to students on the cusp of high school graduation and college entry.

College completion rates have moved to the forefront of U.S. education reform efforts in the 2010s. For an array of reasons, many students do not finish college: fewer than half of the high school class of 2004 earned a college degree within eight years of their intended high school graduation (Lauff & Ingels, 2014). There is now widespread recognition that such a low level of postsecondary attainment is unacceptable. The Lumina and Gates Foundations' funding priorities, Tennessee's Drive to 55 campaign,

NEW DIRECTIONS FOR COMMUNITY COLLEGES, no. 169, Spring 2015 © 2015 Wiley Periodicals, Inc.
Published online in Wiley Online Library (wileyonlinelibrary.com) • DOI: 10.1002/cc.20137

and the Obama administration's postsecondary reform agenda are just a few examples of the focus and ambitious goal setting aimed at ensuring college completion, not just access.

These goals are driven by recognition that high school graduation is no longer sufficient for economic success, both individually and for our nation. Credential completion is associated with significantly higher wages and earnings (Baum, Kurose, & Ma, 2013), increased tax revenues (Rouse, 2007), decreased unemployment (Baum, Ma, & Payea, 2010), and lower rates of criminality and welfare receipt (Baum et al., 2010; Belfield & Bailey, 2011). Yet despite the increased importance of college, the structure of our education system continues to reflect the needs and assumptions of previous generations: high school graduation was seen as sufficient for most, college was only for some, and consequently there was no need to systematically connect the two sectors. High schools and colleges continue to be financed, managed, regulated, and evaluated by separate systems and agencies.

Most reforms aimed at improving college completion focus on the content of education, such as the high school curriculum, but do not fundamentally lessen the divide between the high school and college sectors. The Common Core State Standards, for example, seek to improve college readiness by ensuring that high school graduates have learned the academic and content knowledge and skills necessary for college success. Changed content does not, however, ensure that the two sectors work more closely, and some authors have expressed concern that despite being aimed at college readiness, the postsecondary sector was not systematically involved in the development of the standards (Barnett & Fay, 2013). Similarly, reforming developmental or remedial education within the postsecondary sector may improve the likelihood of individual students completing college by changing what or how entering college students are prepared for college-credit coursework, but this reform does not require cross-sector collaboration (Bailey & Karp, in press). None of these efforts fundamentally alter the ways that high schools and colleges relate to one another, deliver coursework, and engage with students along their paths to college.

Dual enrollment is different because at its core it requires high schools and colleges to interact in ways that bring them closer together, as the chapters in this volume demonstrate. Moreover, though dual enrollment has traditionally been seen as a program that improves high schools (see Bailey, Hughes, & Karp [2002] for further discussion of this rationale), it should also be seen as a strategy for improving college completion. Dual enrollment programs essentially create linkages between the secondary and postsecondary sectors that reduce the fragmentation of the two and create stronger, smoother pathways from high school to college for participating students.

The College Completion Pipeline

The college completion process starts well before students' last years of college. In order to graduate, students must pass through a series of sequential steps. Admittedly, some students do not follow this linear path precisely, and the path as described here is a simplified description of the process. Still, the general outline remains true for the majority of students in our educational system. First, students must gain academic skills and graduate from high school. Then, they must enter college, as one cannot graduate from an institution one never started! Once in college, students must be successful in their courses, persist, and finally complete the requirements for a degree.

The fragmentation of our education systems means that this pipeline leaks at every new transition. For example, according to statistics from the U.S. Department of Education (Aud et al., 2013), 3.1 million students graduated on time from high school in 2010, successfully navigating the first two steps of the completion pipeline. However, only 2.1 million of those enrolled in college the following fall—meaning that nearly one third of them "leaked out" at this third step. Of the 2004 graduates who successfully navigated the college matriculation step of the pipeline, nearly 40% were lost later on, having never completed a postsecondary credential eight years after high school (Lauff & Ingels, 2014).

It is important to recognize that the pipeline is leakier for some types of students than others. For example, while 81% of upper-income high school graduates successfully enter college the following fall, only 52% of low-income students do so—a 29% gap (Aud et al., 2013). The result is a stunning disparity in college graduation rates between students from more- and less-advantaged groups: of the high school class of 2004, 23% of students from the lowest income quartile had earned a college degree by 2012, whereas 67% of students from the highest quartile had done so (Lauff & Ingels, 2014). Similar gaps exist between White and Black or Hispanic students (Aud et al., 2012).

Addressing the Leaky Pipeline: Dual Enrollment as a College Completion Strategy

Dual enrollment is a powerful college completion strategy because it addresses every transition point in the pipeline described above. Rather than merely upgrading the high school curriculum, it provides a comprehensive way to restructure the relationship between secondary and postsecondary institutions. By encouraging closer collaboration and coordination between high schools and colleges, it essentially fuses pieces of the pipeline more closely together, helping students make their way through rather than leaking out at key transition points.

New Directions for Community Colleges • DOI: 10.1002/cc

As the research discussed in the Editors' Notes illustrates, success begins for dual enrollment students in high school when they become academically and behaviorally prepared for college. They navigate each transition more successfully than their nonparticipating peers, graduating from high school at greater rates, entering college, and succeeding once there. Finally, dual enrollment participants are more likely to complete college and earn a postsecondary credential.

Of course, participating in dual enrollment is no guarantee that students will successfully navigate the path into and through postsecondary education, and some dual enrollment students are still lost on the way to a college degree. However, it appears that dual enrollment can influence every point of the college completion pipeline, making it less leaky and easier for students to move along. Given the potential efficacy as a strategy to achieve the nation's completion agenda, it is important for educators and policymakers to understand why these benefits accrue, so that replication efforts best maximize dual enrollment's potential.

Dual Enrollment Is a Structural Reform

Elsewhere, I have argued that one likely mechanism for positive research findings is that dual enrollment students are exposed to and able to practice the norms and expectations of college success (Karp, 2012). At the individual level, this argument still applies. But given the chapters in this volume, I would argue that there is a second, structural dynamic at play. When well implemented, dual enrollment fundamentally changes how education is structured, the relationship between institutions, and even how institutions are organized. Dual enrollment improves our fragmented educational system by streamlining the process of students moving from secondary to postsecondary school.

Hofmann (2012) argues that dual enrollment aids college completion by occupying a "middle space" between high school and college (p. 3). The chapters in this volume demonstrate that dual enrollment may go even further, eliminating the middle space entirely. In well-implemented programs, delivering education to students in the late high school years becomes a collective effort, in which high schools and colleges make decisions jointly, merge policies, and intertwine their teaching, funding, and curricular strategies.

What do I mean by a "structural reform"? Such reforms change how education systems are organized, how systems and institutions relate to one another, and how institutions themselves arrange their work processes and practices. For example, if curricular changes try to patch pipeline leaks by a single institution offering more challenging courses, *structural* changes alter the way that curricula are designed and delivered altogether. A high school can change its curriculum independent of a college; to offer dual enrollment, however, it must work with a college to provide college coursework.

Hanson, Prusha, and Iverson illustrate this point in Chapter 7, discussing the ways that high school teachers, counselors, and administrators perceive curricular changes in their schools as a result of their dual enrollment collaboration with postsecondary partners.

Dual enrollment is a structural reform because colleges and high schools, as well as their respective state and local systems, both have to participate in and *adapt to* a new educational paradigm that fuses secondary and postsecondary education. As a result, educational institutions must redefine their missions and what it means to serve their students: What is a high school senior or a college freshman when students' course taking enrolls them in both types of classes simultaneously? What does it mean for a high school to deliver college coursework? What defines and differentiates college coursework from high school coursework—the location, instructor, students, or content? How does one administer an educational program, including the calendar and criteria for credit earning, when students are enrolled in more than one program at a time?

As Haag illustrates in Chapter 5, these questions are even more challenging for CTE dual enrollment programs. Infusing dual enrollment into CTE programs requires practitioners to rethink the role of college for CTE students, the intended outcomes of CTE programs, and the relationship between high school and college CTE programs. The chapters by Ferguson, Baker, and Burnett (Chapter 8) and Kanny (Chapter 6) also illustrate the ways that dual enrollment partners must rethink support service delivery— usually done by high schools and colleges in isolation—in order to support students who may lack the social and emotional maturity of regularly matriculated college students.

Thus, in dual enrollment programs, philosophical and logistical questions must be jointly negotiated and the resulting answers must be jointly administered. Usually, the solutions require both institutions to modify how they function to make dual enrollment a reality. As a result, there is tighter— though still imperfect—coupling of the secondary and postsecondary sectors, the pipeline gets fused, and gaps disappear or at least get smaller.

Early college high schools and other new accelerated models like P-TECH are the most radical example of this fusion, as Barnett, Maclutsky, and Wagonlander illustrate in Chapter 4. In this model, the gap between high school and college disappears completely as the two types of institutions coexist, essentially creating a new type of institution that is neither exclusively high school nor exclusively college. Less-intensive models, like enhanced dual enrollment systems in Michigan and Smart Scholars programs in New York, still require high schools and colleges to rethink how they deliver coursework and student support services.

Beyond changes to partnering institutions, dual enrollment requires changes to the policy structures governing secondary and postsecondary education. In Chapter 1, Taylor, Borden, and Park illustrate the myriad ways that state policies must redefine the final years of high school. For example, defining dual enrollment eligibility criteria and who is college-ready is a key policy dimension that is important to understand and study. Pretlow and Patteson demonstrate in Chapter 2 that different state policy decisions can influence the ability of dual enrollment to create structural change at the institutional level and, consequently, influence how effectively dual enrollment programs can smooth the path from secondary education to postsecondary completion. Finally, Scheffel, McLemore, and Lowe remind us in Chapter 9 that in this new educational paradigm of merged sectors, even external structures need to be redesigned. Existing accreditation systems at the secondary and postsecondary levels are no longer sufficient for a multisector, multi-institutional mode of course delivery; a new organization, like NACEP, may be required to fill the gap.

Dual Enrollment and the Equity Challenge

The completion agenda is not merely about increasing numbers of college degrees, it is also about ensuring that the historical inequalities in college completion among demographic and economic groups are mitigated. Given the statistics on disparate college completion rates discussed earlier in this chapter, the greater challenge is to ensure that underrepresented minority, first-generation college-going, low-income, and otherwise educationally disadvantaged students are able to achieve college completion rates similar to their more advantaged peers.

The structural changes that dual enrollment brings about appear to be effective in helping underrepresented students navigate the path to college completion. The positive results for dual enrollment participation appear to hold true even for students most at risk of falling through the cracks of the completion pipeline, including males, career and technical education, low-income, first-generation, and minority students (Karp, Calcagno, Hughes, Jeong, & Bailey, 2007; Rodríguez, Hughes, & Belfield, 2012; Struhl & Vargas, 2012).

Navigating a tightly coupled educational system requires students to possess less social and cultural capital than a decoupled system, thereby minimizing one disadvantage held by first-generation college students. Structures that assume all students will attend college create conditions for college aspirations and preparation that include, rather than exclude, disadvantaged and underrepresented students. In Chapter 3, Roach, Gamez Vargas, and David illustrate the success low-income students can have when high schools and colleges work together to break boundaries and provide access to dual enrollment for students previously denied the opportunity to participate.

Ensuring that dual enrollment programs effectively meet the equity challenge is not easy, however. As Kanny points out in Chapter 6, providing underrepresented and first-generation college-going students access to dual enrollment programs can be a mixed blessing, with unintended negative consequences. Dual enrollment needs to be implemented carefully, with clear messages to students about expectations and consequences for failure, as well as strong supports and guidance.

State policy has an important role to play in ensuring that dual enrollment addresses the equity gap. Some policies can be exclusionary, thereby subverting transition efforts for underrepresented students. Eligibility, transportation, and funding policies are among the relevant policies that if designed or written incorrectly can serve as barriers to participation for low-income, disadvantaged students (Hughes, Rodríguez, Edwards, & Belfield, 2012). The chapters in this volume addressing state policy illustrate the many ways that policies can inhibit, rather than amplify, dual enrollment's potential to increase equity in postsecondary attainment rates. Transfer policies are particularly important, as the ability to apply dual enrollment credit to future degrees is a key mechanism by which low-income students can leverage dual enrollment experiences toward future degree attainment. Taylor and his colleagues in Chapter 1 find that half of states do not have policies addressing the transfer of dual enrollment credit, so this is a policy area that appears ripe for further attention.

Conclusion

Research indicates that dual enrollment has a positive influence on students' access to and success in college. Dual enrollment therefore has an important role to play in helping the nation meet its completion goals. Importantly, dual enrollment can help ensure equity in college completion, not just higher overall completion rates.

Dual enrollment appears to improve student outcomes by simultaneously changing individuals' educational experiences and spurring structural change. By encouraging high schools and colleges to more closely couple their educational processes, dual enrollment lessens the gap between two traditionally separate sectors of our education system. In doing so, it fuses the gaps in the completion pipeline, helping more students move from one sector to the other. Reconceptualizing dual enrollment as a structural reform helps us understand why it is both so challenging to administer yet so promising.

Placing dual enrollment in the context of the college completion agenda raises its profile as an education reform. No longer is it solely a high school enrichment program; rather, it becomes a tool in the larger effort to ensure that all U.S. students have the opportunity to obtain a college credential. This rationale can help administrators shore up support for their programs by reminding skeptics that dual enrollment is part of a larger enterprise. That it is effective for students most disadvantaged within our current system only makes this argument more compelling.

Reconceptualizing dual enrollment as a structural strategy may also encourage administrators, policymakers, and even instructors to "think big."

Rather than working to administer a single program at their school, individuals should consider ways to engage dual enrollment with other college readiness and completion efforts, such as senior year transition courses, early warning assessments, or college bridge programs. Moreover, dual enrollment stakeholders can and should engage in policy-related conversations about how best to structure, incentivize, and administer dual enrollment and other college completion initiatives.

Finally, as pundits and policymakers think about ways to "remake," "reenvision," or "reengineer" the "high schools and colleges of the future," dual enrollment provides a model of what such new forms of schooling might look like. By fusing secondary and postsecondary education, and successfully leveraging this fusion to smooth students' pathways to completion, dual enrollment programs demonstrate the potential efficacy of a new, more streamlined educational system. Dual enrollment creates a compelling argument in favor of changing not just curriculum- or classroom-level practices, but entire educational structures to potentially better meet the needs of today's students and the modern economy.

Dual enrollment is not a magic bullet for college completion. But there is evidence that it is an important strategy for helping the nation meet its completion goals. It does so by moving the structure of schooling away from isolated institutions to more connected and collaborative ones, therefore eliminating some of the interinstitutional gaps that get in the way of so many students' college aspirations. It also reminds us that improving educational outcomes will require changing the structure, not just the content, of schooling in the United States.

References

Aud, S., Hussar, W., Johnson, F., Kena, G., Roth, E., Manning, E., . . . Zhang, J. (2012). *The condition of education 2012* (NCES 2012-033). Washington, DC: National Center for Education Statistics, U.S. Department of Education. Retrieved from http://nces.ed.gov/pubs2012/2012045_4.pdf

Aud, S., Wilkinson-Flicker, S., Kristapovich, P., Rathbun, A., Wang, X., & Zhang, J. (2013). *The condition of education 2013* (NCES 2013-037). Washington, DC: National Center for Education Statistics, U.S. Department of Education. Retrieved from http://nces.ed.gov/pubsearch/pubsinfo.asp?pubid=2013037

Bailey, T. B., Hughes, K. L., & Karp, M. M. (2002). *What role can dual enrollment programs play in easing the transition between high school and postsecondary education?* New York, NY: Community College Research Center/Institute on Education and the Economy.

Bailey, T. B., & Karp, M. M. (in press). Bridging the high school-college divide. In S. Ladd & P. Goertz (Eds.), *Handbook of research in education finance and policy.* New York, NY: Routledge.

Barnett, E. A., & Fay, M. P. (2013). *The common core state standards: Implications for community colleges and student preparedness for college* (NCPR Working Paper). New York, NY: National Center for Postsecondary Research.

Baum, S., Kurose, C., & Ma, J. (2013). *How college shapes lives: Understanding the issues.* New York, NY: The College Board Advocacy and Policy Center.

Baum, S., Ma, J., & Payea, K. (2010). *Education pays: The benefits of higher education for individuals and society*. New York, NY: The College Board Advocacy and Policy Center.

Belfield, C. R., & Bailey, T. (2011). The benefits of attending community college: A review of the evidence. *Community College Review, 39*(1), 46–68.

Hofmann, E. (2012). Why dual enrollment? In E. Hofmann & D. Voloch (Eds.), *New Directions for Higher Education: No. 158. Dual enrollment: Strategies, outcomes, and lessons for school-college partnerships* (pp. 1–8). San Francisco, CA: Jossey-Bass.

Hughes, K. L., Rodríguez, O., Edwards, L., & Belfield, C. (2012). *Broadening the benefits of dual enrollment: Reaching underachieving and underrepresented students with career-focused programs*. New York, NY: Community College Research Center, Teachers College, Columbia University.

Karp, M. M. (2012). "I don't know, I've never been to college!" Dual enrollment as a college readiness strategy. In E. Hofmann & D. Voloch (Eds.), *New Directions for Higher Education: No. 158. Dual enrollment: Strategies, outcomes, and lessons for school-college partnerships* (pp. 21–28). San Francisco, CA: Jossey-Bass.

Karp, M. M., Calcagno, J. C., Hughes, K. L., Jeong, D. W., & Bailey, T. (2007). *The postsecondary achievement of participants in dual enrollment: An analysis of student outcomes in two states*. St. Paul, MN: National Research Center for Career and Technical Education, University of Minnesota.

Lauff, E., & Ingels, S. J. (2014). *Education Longitudinal Study of 2002 (ELS:2002): A first look at 2002 high school sophomores 10 years later* (NCES 2014-363). Washington, DC: National Center for Education Statistics, U.S. Department of Education. Retrieved from http://nces.ed.gov/pubsearch/pubsinfo.asp?pubid=2014363

Rodríguez, O., Hughes, K. L., & Belfield, C. (2012). *Bridging college and careers: Using dual enrollment to enhance career and technical education pathways* (NCPR Working Paper). New York, NY: National Center for Postsecondary Research.

Rouse, C. E. (2007). Consequences for the labor market. In C. R. Belfield & H. M. Levin (Eds.), *The price we pay: Economic and social consequences of an inadequate education* (pp. 99–124). Washington, DC: The Brookings Institution.

Struhl, B., & Vargas, J. (2012). *Taking college courses in high school: A strategy for college readiness*. Boston, MA: Jobs for the Future.

MELINDA MECHUR KARP *is assistant director for staff and institutional development at the Community College Research Center at Teachers College, Columbia University.*

INDEX